Exciting new reso

MW00478169

Thank you for an overwhelming *Essentials You Always Wanted to Know: 3rd Edition*. We are committed to publishing books that are content-rich, concise and approachable enabling more readers to read and make the fullest use of them.

We are excited to announce two major add-ons in this new (4th) edition of the book.

- A Chapter Summary is added at the end of every chapter. This will help to get a quick access point of what was covered in the chapter. It also assists in identifying the important information afterreading through the entire chapter.

- This updated edition includes detailed and self-explanatory solutions to unsolved examples in Practice Exercises. You may download the solutions at www.vibrantpublishers.com

Should you have any questions or suggestions, feel free to email us at reachus@vibrantpublishers.com

We hope this book provides you the most enriching learning experience.

THIS BOOK IS AVAILABLE IN E-BOOK, PAPERBACK(B/W) AND PAPERBACK (COLOR) FORMAT.

angela Wheaton 239-9796 (handwritten)

Books in
Self-Learning Management Series

Cost Accounting and Management
Essentials You Always
Wanted To Know
ISBN: 978-1-949395-35-8

Financial Accounting
Essentials You Always
Wanted To Know
ISBN: 978-1-949395-32-7

Project Management
Essentials You Always
Wanted To Know
ISBN: 978-1-949395-39-6

Financial Management
Essentials You Always
Wanted To Know
ISBN: 978-1-949395-37-2

Principles of Management
Essentials You Always
Wanted To Know
ISBN: 978-1-946383-93-8

Business Strategy
Essentials You Always
Wanted To Know
ISBN: 978-1-946383-98-3

Marketing Management
Essentials You Always
Wanted To Know
ISBN: 978-1-949395-04-4

Operations and Supply Chain
Management Essentials You
Always Wanted To Know
ISBN: 978-1-949395-24-2

For the most updated list of books visit
www.vibrantpublishers.com

PROJECT MANAGEMENT

ESSENTIALS YOU ALWAYS WANTED TO KNOW

FOURTH EDITION

KALPESH ASHAR

VIBRANT
PUBLISHERS

Project Management

Essentials You Always Wanted To Know
Fourth Edition

ISBN-10: 1-949395-39-1
ISBN-13: 978-1-949395-39-6
Library of Congress Control Number: 2012916200

Vibrant Publishers books are available at special quantity discount for sales promotions, or for use in corporate training programs. For more information please write to **bulkorders@vibrantpublishers.com**

Please email feedback / corrections (technical, grammatical or spelling) to **spellerrors@vibrantpublishers.com**

To access the complete catalogue of Vibrant Publishers, visit **www.vibrantpublishers.com**

Table of Contents

About the Author

Kalpesh Ashar is a management consultant and corporate trainer holding an MBA (Dean's Award Winner) from SPJIMR, one of Asia's top business schools, and an Engineering degree with honors in Electronics. He has over 21 years of experience in large organizations and start-ups in Asia, USA, and Europe. Kalpesh has worked in several project management roles, like Senior Project Manager, Delivery Manager, and Program Manager. He is passionate about writing on management subjects. His techno-business background gives him a unique position to write on management topics that are easy to understand for non-MBA graduates. His books are authored in a simple to understand manner without unnecessary use of management jargons.

Other contributors

We would like to sincerely thank Brodie Schultz for providing solutions to all the practice exercises that were unsolved till the previous editions of this book. Brodie is a young aspiring engineer currently divulging in the areas of marketing, financial management, and innovative manufacturing processes at Ford Motor Company and has received his Masters of Business Administration and Bachelor of Science in Mechanical Engineering.Brodie is also an active board member for his local Penn State Alumni Association Chapter, an avid cook, fisherman, and golfer.

This page is intentionally left blank

Helpful Templates

The following Templates will help you manage projects more efficiently:

1. Activity Sequences
2. Cost Budgeting
3. Issues Log
4. Project Charter
5. Project Scope Statement
6. RACI Matrix – RAM
7. Requirements Document
8. Risk Register
9. Stakeholder Register
10. WBS Dictionary

To download these templates, visit www.vibrantpublishers.com and check the *Additional resources* section of this book.

This page is intentionally left blank

Chapter **1**

Project Management Overview

Projects have, today, become an integral part of our everyday life; may it be at work or at home. All changes in business and in personal life are brought about by projects.

Although projects have been executed for several centuries now, it is only much recently that a need has been felt to manage projects using a scientific approach. This approach ensures greater chances of success but cannot guarantee it. Much still lies in how the project manager is able to apply these concepts to a particular project in the most effective way. Knowing the concepts in project management and their practical application to real-life projects is the starting point for any project manager. This book provides this knowledge and skills and is written in a way that should be easy to understand for both experienced project managers and those with little or no experience in project management.

Project Definition

We use the word Project to describe various types of work. However, all of them have at least two things in common:

a) Start and End/Timeline

b) Unique Outcome

Every project needs to have a planned start date and a planned end date. A project cannot carry on forever. Every project also delivers something that is unique or different than the outcome of any other project. It is possible to deliver similar things but not the same thing. The output can be a product, service, or a combination of both.

As per Project Management Institute (PMI®), project is defined as *"A temporary endeavor undertaken to create a unique product, service, or result"*.

The above definition of project is actually quite wide in nature and covers everything that has a timeline and differentiable outcome. Some examples of projects at work are:

a) New product development

b) Enhancement in existing product

c) Market research

d) Feasibility study

e) Developing a software application

f) Constructing a building

Some examples of projects in personal life are:

a) Wedding event management

b) Planning a birthday party

c) Vacation planning and bookings

d) Home improvement

If the above are examples of a project, then what are the works that are not categorized as projects called? They are called Operations. They are repetitive in nature where similar activities are performed on a regular basis. Some examples of operations are:

a) Manufacturing unit's assembly line

b) Cleaning a building everyday

c) Regular maintenance of servers, and other electrical equipment

Reasons for Starting a Project

Projects are started with one or more reasons. Each project has certain objectives or goals to achieve. These goals have to be linked with the organisation's strategic goals and will generally provide a boost to the company's top line (revenues) or help in reduction of costs and, hence, in increasing the bottom line (profit).

Some projects may also be required due to mandatory regulations, or due to corporate social responsibility (CSR) activities that every company undertakes these days. Below are some reasons for starting a project:

a) **Market/Consumer demand** – Project that led to development of Apple's iPod

b) **Technology change** – Project that led to introduction of 3G mobile services

c) **Statutory/legal/social mandate** – Project that implemented telecom regulatory requirements, like Number Portability

d) **Internal organisational need** – Project that implements a new process for procurement within the company

Project Management

Every project is started with an intention of meeting certain objectives. When one applies his/her knowledge, skills and tools and techniques to manage a project in order to achieve these objectives, it is called Project Management.

Although it is generally felt that only the project manager does project management, it is usually not true. Every person working on a project is performing activities that help in achieving the project's objectives. Hence, every team member does project management, albeit in lesser proportion than the project manager. This is because team members also perform technical work on the project apart from project management.

Program and Portfolio

Projects are either independent of each other or related to each other. The ones that are related need to be managed in a co-ordinated way. For example, construction of a building can be divided into various projects, like civil work, plumbing work, electrical work, interior work etc., as each of these require different skills. However, all these projects are closely related and cannot be managed completely independent of each other. In such cases, we put the projects in a Program. A Program is a collection of related projects that helps in managing them in a better way. There is generally a Program Manager who performs this job of managing the relationship between projects. The individual projects have their Project Manager who is responsible for managing the individual projects.

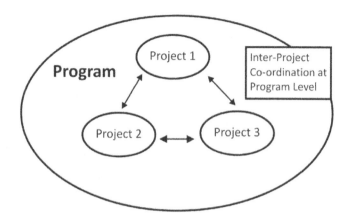

A Portfolio is a collection of all work being done (projects, programs, operations) with the same strategic objectives. Most companies designate a person for a large customer account. Several call this person an Account Manager. All projects that are performed for that particular customer are clubbed together and the Account Manager represents them to the customer. Several companies working in various geographies do the classification on the basis of regions, like Americas, Europe, Middle East & Africa, Asia Pacific etc. In such a case, all projects carried out for a particular geography are represented by a Region/Country Manager for that geography. Whatever be the way to define this engagement, they have one thing in common – strategic objectives for the portfolio of projects. The generic term used for such a person representing all work done against common strategic objectives is Portfolio Manager and the projects are said to be part of a Portfolio.

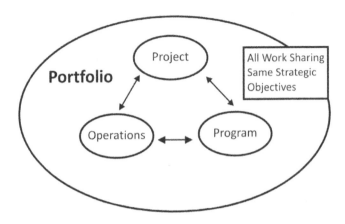

The importance of Portfolio comes from the fact that Portfolio Managers are given targets for the quarter/year by the senior management of the company. These targets can be based on revenue increase, market share, profit margin, resource utilization etc. The Portfolio Manager needs to ensure that all the projects falling under the portfolio are working towards achieving these objectives. A Portfolio may contain Programs and even any Operations being carried out apart from Projects.

Project Management Office (PMO)

Today, most companies that execute several projects have a centralized department called Project Management Office (PMO). However, the work performed by the PMO differs. It generally depends upon the size of the company and whether the company's main business is into projects or operations. Some companies, like auto manufacturers, are mainly into the operations business. Others, like infrastructure companies, are mainly into the projects business.

Consider a start-up company that does project work. Such a company may not have a PMO and the few projects are managed by the project managers in a way that the individual project managers think best. As this company matures into a small-sized company, several projects are carried out and a need is felt to manage projects in a standardized way. This is when a PMO is established, generally with a single person running the show. This person, called the PMO, provides standards, policies, processes and templates to manage projects and the project managers are expected to follow these guidelines.

When this company matures into a medium-sized company, even more projects are performed, and new project managers are hired. Then there is a need to train, coach, and mentor the project managers and also provide centralized project reporting (generally referred to as MIS reporting – Management Information System) to senior management. This additional responsibility is then taken up by the PMO which now becomes a full-fledged department.

When the company further grows in size, it may opt for a more active PMO that takes complete responsibility of managing all projects in the company. Every time a new project begins, one person from the PMO department is assigned to it as a project manager. The PMO head now functions as a manager of project managers. However, this kind of PMO works best when the company does projects in the same technical field or domain, so any project can be assigned to any project manager.

Management by Objectives (MBO)

Companies set targets that they must achieve in the financial year. These apply directly to the senior management of the company.

They then set targets for their sub-ordinates that help in achieving the company's target. This continues to the lowest level in the company where everybody has targets and if all of them achieve them then the company is able to achieve its targets. This way of managing a company is known as Management by Objectives (MBO).

MBO is a top-down approach wherein, the targets are first finalized at the senior management level and later on get refined as they are given to the lower levels of the company. Every individual gets targets that are based on the company's targets. For MBO to work, the senior management has to provide support and should believe in the targets. The targets have to be measurable and achievable. Below are the three stages involved in MBO:

a) Setting of unambiguous and realistic targets/objectives

b) Periodically evaluating if the targets are being met

c) Implementing corrective action, if required, to bring performance in line with the targets

Companies generally formalize this process in their performance appraisal system. During the beginning of the year, targets are set for each and every employee of the company in a top-down fashion. Later on, the performance is evaluated every quarter or at the end of half year to see if the targets are being met. This is generally done through a mid-term review process where managers give subjective feedback to sub-ordinates. Any deviations are corrected by taking appropriate action. Then, at the end of the year, the employees are appraised objectively to verify how well they have met the objectives.

Constraints

Every project is managed within certain limitations. The project manager has to keep these factors in mind while planning and executing the project. These factors are called Constraints. Every project has six constraints given below:

a) **Scope** – The project needs to deliver a certain scope and also manage changes to scope in order to succeed. Scope is the part that says what the project needs to deliver. A project's scope is arrived at from the project's requirements.

b) **Time** – The project needs to complete within a stipulated timeframe

c) **Cost/Budget** – The project needs to be done within the stipulated budget

d) **Resources** – The work on the project depends a lot on available resources – human resources, machinery, and raw materials

e) **Quality** – The product of the project will only be accepted provided it is within a given range of defined quality parameters

f) **Risk** – Several uncertainties exist that could come in the way of successful project completion that the project manager needs to manage

The above constraints compete against each other and a project manager needs to juggle between them or perform a trade-off. For example, if the scope of the project is increased, it could affect time, cost, resources, quality, and risk on the project. Based on the evaluation of these impacts a decision will be made on whether the scope addition should be included or not. Similarly, if the customer wants an early delivery (changing time constraint), then it could have an impact on scope, cost, resources, quality, and risk on the project.

Stakeholders

Projects are done in order to deliver to the requirements. These requirements come from various stakeholders of the project. Stakeholders are those individuals and organisations that are impacted by the outcome of the project. They will also include those who work on the project, like the project manager and the project team members. The list below gives examples of stakeholders:

a) **Sponsor** – one who pays for the project

b) **Customer** – one who takes delivery of the project's product

c) **End user** – one who uses the product of the project

d) **Project Manager**

e) **Project Team**

f) **Performing organisation** – company executing the project

g) **Government/statutory bodies** – in case any approvals are to be taken

h) **Environmental/Social/Political groups** – if the project infringes on the group's objective

i) **Society as a whole** – companies and projects are done within our society and hence, have responsibility towards the society

Stakeholder Management is extremely important for success of a project. It includes the following:

a) Identifying stakeholders

b) Capturing stakeholders' requirements and expectations

c) Managing stakeholders' influence

d) Communicating with stakeholders

All the above responsibilities finally rest with the project manager, with the first one, i.e. Identify stakeholders, being the most critical. If a project misses identifying a stakeholder, then it may lead to changes being asked at later stages in the project. It happens when a stakeholder who was not identified earlier comes to know that the project would impact him/her and put forth their requirements from the project. We often call this Scope Creep.

Organisational Structures

Every organisation defines its own unique structure. However, all the structures are based on three underlying structures, using which every company creates its own unique structure. The structure largely depends upon the kind of business the company is into. Manufacturing companies will have a different structure than Consulting companies. Similarly, companies into production would define their structure that will be different than companies into services. Let us first see the three basic blocks using which structures are formed.

Functional Organisation

This structure is based on functions or departments. Each department possesses a unique skill, like marketing, production, procurement etc. Each function is led by a Functional Manager, who is the decision making authority in the company. This kind of structure has very few projects that only run within the function. There are no cross-functional projects. This structure is depicted in the diagram below:

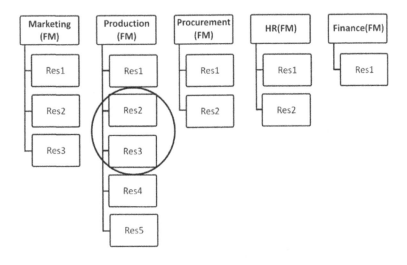

In the above structure, all resources are owned by a particular function and they perform functional work. Some resources may also be involved in projects, like Res 2 and Res 3 in production function. They report to the functional manager of production function for both their functional work as well as for their project work. All decision making authority lies with the functional manager. Role of a project manager in this structure is restricted to mere following the instructions given by the functional manager, who does most of the project management in the company. For example, a manufacturing company would have a production department/function. All employees belonging to this function would do production related work. If the function wants to investigate ways to improve their productivity, then some employees would be picked up and given additional responsibility to make a report on productivity improvement initiatives as part of a project. There would be one person designated as the project manager who would be looking after the day-to-day activities on the project, but the functional manager would take decisions related to the project. The project manager is merely acting as a person who gets the job done but does not have authority to take any project related decisions.

This structure is most suited to those companies whose main job is not projects but operations and who don't have a need to perform any cross-functional projects.

Matrix Organisation

This structure is derived from a functional organisation. It allows for cross-functional projects and provides greater decision making authority to project managers. It looks similar to the functional organisation as shown below:

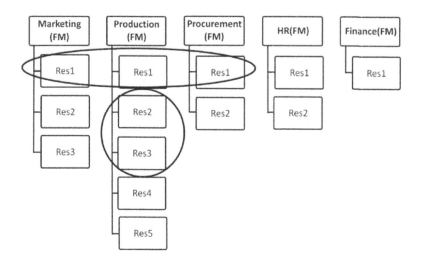

In the above structure there is an additional project shown that runs across three functions – marketing, production, and procurement. The resources working in such projects would now have to report to multiple bosses – their functional manager and the project manager for the project they work in. Hence, communication in such a structure might be complex. This structure allows for most of the decision making authority, with the functional manager or with the project manager. In cases where the project manager does not have much decision making authority we call them project co-ordinators or project expeditors instead of project managers. For example, consider an auto manufacturing company. Although their main business is to manufacture cars, they need to initiate projects for making improvement to existing car models or to conceptualize a new car model. Such projects would need involvement from various functions, like marketing, R&D, production, finance etc. In such a case a cross-functional project would be initiated and the organisational structure would be a matrix. It is then up to the company to decide how much authority is to be given to the project managers.

Companies who do not have projects as their main business but need to often run cross-functional projects or those who need to build capability in certain functional areas would prefer this kind of organisational structure.

Projectised Organisation

This structure contains only projects within the company. There are no functions. Hence, there are no functional manager; only project managers. All resources work on projects and report to the project manager as shown below:

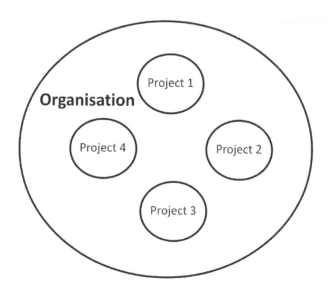

As there are no functions, this structure has project specific resources and capability building could be more difficult. This is because there are "islands" of knowledge. Once a project has been completed, the project resources are either absorbed in other projects or are released from the company as they are not owned by any function. This is termed as "no home". Project managers have complete authority to take project decisions. Companies whose main job is to perform projects would prefer this kind of structure

In reality, most modern organisations use a combination of these three organisational structures. Those who are into projects would have most part of the organisation as projectised but also maintain some functions to build capability or for support functions, like finance and HR. Such combinations are termed as a Composite Organisational structure.

Lifecycles

Every product (or service) has a life cycle. Every project also has a life cycle. These two life cycles are different. A product (or service) life cycle has the following stages – Start-up, rapid growth, maturity and decline. Every product (or service) is launched at the start-up phase when the market demand and knowledge about the product is low. Slowly the demand picks up as more people know about the product and we reach the second stage of the life cycle – rapid growth. Then, most of the people possess the product and there are very few new sales and a few replacement sales. This is the maturity stage. Finally, due to innovation or technological advance, the product is replaced by a new one and the sales start declining. This life cycle stays the same for every product or service and is depicted in the graph below:

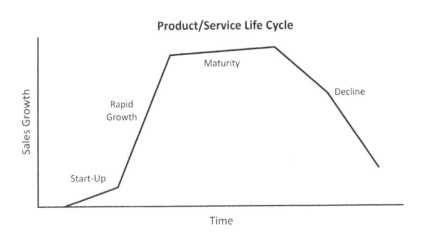

Product/Service Life Cycle

As against a standard product life cycle, projects follow different life cycles based on the industry and company they are performed in. For example, the life cycle followed in the software industry could be – requirements gathering, high-level design, detailed design, implementation, unit testing, integration testing, user acceptance testing, go-live. In the construction industry the project life cycle could be – planning, design, mobilisation, construction, demobilisation, handover. Many a times we also refer to the project life cycle as project phases, and these depend upon the industry.

Project Management Phases

Every project goes through five project management phases. It starts with Initiation, followed by Planning, Execution, Monitoring & Control, and Closure. Monitoring & Control happens in parallel with the other phases and helps monitor the particular phase and take appropriate control action, called corrective or preventive action.

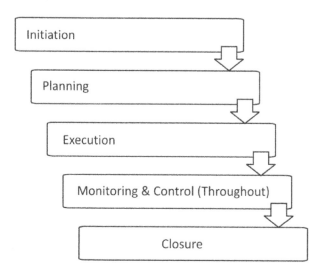

The phases may not always happen one after the other. There is a certain degree of overlap between phases. Monitoring & Control is a phase that starts almost in the beginning of the project and goes almost till the end of the project. Execution phase is generally the one that takes most amount of time and consumes most amounts of resources and, hence, incurs most of the project budget.

The next set of chapters describes the project management phases one by one along with what happens in each of them. Most of the text follows the processes described in PMBOK® (Project Management Body of Knowledge) issued by PMI® (Project Management Institute). It contains the industry best practices in project management.

Solved Examples

1.1 Which ones of the following is a project:
   a) Bulk manufacturing a part of a car
   b) Construction of a bridge
   c) Filling forms in a bank's back office
   d) Running daily jobs on a computer database

Solution:

Construction of a bridge is a project. All others are operations as they are repetitive in nature.

1.2 What is the difference between a Project, Program, and a Portfolio?

Solution:

A Project is a set of interrelated tasks carried out within a stipulated timeframe to achieve a unique objective. A Program is a set of interrelated projects. A Portfolio is a set of project, programs, and operations, all of which are tied to the same strategic goals.

1.3 Which organisational structure is the most appropriate for using in a company that has projects as its main business?

Solution:

Projectised organisational structure is the most appropriate for a projects company. This is because the project manager has all the decision making authority on a project. Company's managers would be able to take decisions that are in the best interest of the project and, hence, the company.

Practice Exercise

1.1 Which of the following is not a reason for starting a project?

a) Increasing market share

b) Development of a new product

c) Interest of managers of the company

d) Identification of cost saving initiatives

1.2 Identify key stakeholders from the list below:

a) Customer

b) Sponsor

c) Project Manager of another project in a different program

d) Impacted person with only a minor impact

e) Team Member

f) Government official who does not have much interest or power on the project

1.3 Describe the activities that happen during the five project management phases – Initiation, Planning, Execution, Monitoring & Control, Closure.

1.4 Which one of the six project constraints is the most important? Why? Is that true for all projects?

Chapter Summary

◆ A project has a timeline associated with it, and it creates a unique outcome. Projects are started with a goal in mind, that either add business benefit, or because the work is mandatory.

◆ Program is a collection of interrelated projects. Portfolio clubs all the work together that share the same strategic objectives.

◆ Project Management Office (PMO) is a centralized department that works towards project management excellence in the organization.

◆ Management By Objectives (MBO) is done by setting realistic goals, tracking against these, and taking appropriate preventive and corrective actions, if we are off-track.

◆ Limitations are called constraints. Projects usually have six constraints – scope, time, cost, quality, risks, and resources.

◆ Stakeholders are those who are impacted by the outcome of the project, as well as those who have the ability to influence the project. Stakeholder Management includes identification of stakeholders, documenting requirements and expectations, managing stakeholders' influence, and communicating with stakeholders.

◆ Organizations are divided based on three structures – functional, matrix, and projectized. Functional organization is divided based on functions, with intra-functional projects. Matrix extends a functional organization to include cross-functional projects.

◆ Projectized organizations have only projects within them.

◆ Product Life-cycle starts with Startup, followed by Rapid Growth, Maturity, and then Decline. Project Management Phases in a project are Initiation, Planning, Execution, Monitoring & Control, and Closure.

Chapter **2**

Project Initiation

When a company decides the strategy for the year, it identifies several projects that will help it achieve the goals for the year. However, not all projects may bring business benefits. Hence, the first step is to do project selection and select only those projects that have a business case or are mandatory in nature.

Project Selection

Projects are selected using Project Selection Methods. Generally, many of these methods are applied together and no single method is used alone. Some of the methods are qualitative, whereas, others are quantitative. Below is a list of qualitative criteria used in evaluation of projects:

a) Brand image/market value of the firm

b) Complementary products/services

c) Extension of existing portfolio of products/services

d) Competitive landscape

In order to use the quantitative methods, one needs to estimate the cash flows that the product will need and generate over a period of time. Based on this data we need to calculate the DCF (discounted cash flow) of those future cash flows in today's terms and see if the returns are greater than the cost of capital. For example, if the project will need money to be borrowed from banks @10%, then the cash flows should generate a return that is greater than 10%. Else, the project is going to lose money for the company. Let's assume that the company has estimated the cash flows given below for this project:

Year 0	Year 1	Year 2	Year 3
-$10 million	$2 million	$4 million	$6 million

Just by looking at the above cash flows we might be tempted to select this project as the total cash inflow is $2 million (-$10 + $2 + $4 + $6). However, we need to understand that these cash flows are at different times. Hence, we need to discount them to bring them to their current value using a discounting rate which is equal to the cost of capital. As we have taken a bank loan @10%, we shall discount all these cash flows by 10% per year to get the below DCF using the formula $DCF = \text{Cash flow}/(1 + r)^n$, where r is the cost of capital and n is the number of years.

Year 0	Year 1	Year 2	Year 3
-$10 million	$1.818 million	$3.306 million	$4.508 million

Now it is possible to add the above cash flows to get an idea of project's viability. It turns out that the net cash flow is -$0.368 million. This shows that the project's returns are lower than the cost of capital, so the company will lose money if it invests in this project.

The final net cash flow of -$0.368 is called the NPV (Net Present value) of the project and is one of the most important parameters looked at when making project selection. The higher the NPV the better it is from a quantitative point of view. An NPV of at least 0 is required to provide the returns expected by the company.

A measure similar to NPV is called IRR (Internal Rate of Return) which gives the returns of the project in percentage terms. A project will make money if the IRR is above the cost of capital. For example, if there are two projects, one with an IRR of 15%, other with an IRR of 20% and the cost of capital is 10%, both projects will make money. In such a case if the company wants to select only one project then it would select the second one as it brings in greater returns.

Project Charter

Once the company selects the projects that it will do, it gives authorization for those projects. For this it will issue a Project Charter for each project. The Project Charter is a one or two page document that is issued by the Sponsor of the project. It may have the following contents:

a) Project Name and Description

b) Business need of the project

c) Justification for starting the project

d) High Level requirements

e) Deliverables

f) Constraints

g) Assumptions

h) High Level risks

i) Project Manager

j) Stakeholders

This document authorizes a project manager to apply the company's resources to do the project. Below is a sample Project Charter for a cost reduction project:

PROJECT CHARTER

Project Name

R&D Cost Optimization

Project Description

This project will identify the areas where costs can be optimized to bring about an overall cost reduction in the R&D department without affecting its operations

Business Need

Due to a market slowdown it is imperative that we reduce our costs

Project Justification

Our company spends about 25% of its costs on R&D department. A cost reduction in this department can help us increase our net income by a percentage that is higher than the increase in our revenue after removing the project costs. As per estimates, this project would bring us cost reduction of about 5% and this would increase our net income by 10% with a 5% increase in revenue this year.

High-level Requirements

a) Identify areas of cost reduction in R&D department

b) Suggest ways of implementing cost reduction in the R&D department

Deliverables

a) Report on areas of cost reduction and ways of implementing them in R&D department

b) High-level implementation schedule

Constraints

a) The project should be completed within 2 months

b) The total project cost should not exceed $20,000

Assumptions

a) All required data will be available from the R&D department

b) The cost reduction will not reduce employee productivity

High-level Risks

a) Unavailability of relevant data

b) Unwillingness to part with relevant data

Project Manager

Lan Pham

Stakeholders

a) R&D Functional Manager

b) Marketing Director

Identification of Stakeholders

Once the Project Manager receives the Project Charter the next thing to do is to identify the project's stakeholders. Although the project charter contains a list of stakeholders it may not be a complete list. It is only the view of the sponsor. This is needed so that the project manager can know who are the people giving the requirements and who he needs to communicate with and manage.

This stage is extremely important because if a stakeholder is not identified at this stage then the project could see too many scope changes later on because some stakeholders were not adequately involved in the beginning. In the worst case, if a key stakeholder is missed, then the project could get shelved at a later stage.

A stakeholder register is prepared along with strategy of managing the stakeholders as shown below:

ID	Name	Organization	Contact Info	Role	Main Expectations	Management Strategy

Each stakeholder is put in the above register with a unique ID and respective management strategy. The strategy to manage a stakeholder depends upon two factors – interest in project and power to influence the project. A Power-Interest grid is made as shown below and each stakeholder is mapped in one of the four quadrants. Each quadrant specifies a different management strategy.

Solved Examples

2.1 Describe the main use of a Project Charter.

Solution:

A Project Charter authorizes the start of a project. A project does not exist without a Project Charter. It also authorizes a Project Manager to run the project.

2.2 Which of the below documents includes stakeholder management strategy?

a) Project Charter

b) Stakeholder Register

c) Project Plan

d) Stakeholder List

Solution:

Stakeholder Register

2.3 Which stakeholders would require a "Manage Closely" strategy?

Solution:

A stakeholder that has High Interest in the project and also has High power to Influence the project would require a "Manage Closely" strategy. The project manager would keep in touch with these stakeholders more frequently, asking for their opinions and presenting project progress. These are often the key stakeholders of the project who have a large role to play in project success or failure.

Practice Exercise

2.1 Why is Project Justification included in the Project Charter?

2.2 Who is authorized to issue the Project Charter? Why?

2.3 A project is running without a Project Charter. Which of the below choices are best for the project manager to take in such a situation?

a) Go slow on the project
b) Start planning the project but do not execute it
c) Stop the project as it does not have authorization
d) Execute the project as it is required

2.4 What happens if stakeholder identification is not done properly or skipped altogether?

Solutions to the above questions can be downloaded from the **Online Resources** *section of this book on* **www.vibrantpublishers.com**

Chapter Summary
◆ Projects have to provide business benefits. Hence, they are selected based on certain quantitative and qualitative parameters.
◆ The most popular quantitative project selection methods are Net Present Value (NPV) and Internal Rate of Return (IRR). An NPV > 0 shows a project that is worth taking. A higher value of NPV is preferred. An IRR > Hurdle Rate (Cost of Capital) is required to a take up a project. A higher value of IRR is preferred.
◆ Project Charter is a document that is signed by the Sponsor and issued to the Project Manager to formally authorize a project. It gives a summary of the project.
◆ Stakeholder Identification is done as soon as the project is authorized using a Project Charter. Stakeholder information is captured in a Stakeholder Register. Power-Interest grid is used to decide stakeholder priority.

Chapter 3

Project Planning

Once a project is initiated it goes into the planning stage. During this stage we prepare the project plan for the project. The project plan gives details of how the project will be executed, monitored and controlled.

Planning starts with the Scope where it is decided what needs to be done. It is followed by Time planning where we decide how we will deliver the scope and how much time that would take. Then we estimate the detailed cost of the project work which is followed by planning quality, human resource and communication requirements. Finally, the various risks on the project are identified and managed and procurement documents are created in case the project will be buying any products or services from outside vendors/suppliers/sub-contractors.

Scope Planning

In order for us to deliver a project, the first and the most important thing to know is what the scope of the product is. The product scope includes the features and characteristics of the product that will be the outcome of the project.

Scope Planning is one of the most critical areas because all other planning areas depend upon it. If some scope is missed out or defined incorrectly or ambiguously, then the entire plan would be incorrect and may have to be redone later on. This could lead to huge time and cost overrun on the project.

Scope planning is one area that might work differently for different kinds of projects. Some projects are simply given a project charter with high-level requirements and then the detailed scope is planned. Some other projects are won through competitive bidding. In such projects, detailed scope is already planned before the project is given. This is generally seen in those industries where projects are won through tenders. Although scope planning is done in both types of projects in the same way, it is only the timing that is different.

As an example, take a software development project where competitive bidding for repeat orders from the same customer is not the norm. In such projects, the customer issues a project charter and expects the IT solution provider to do entire scope planning as shown in the diagram below:

As against that, consider a construction project where tenders are floated. The tender document contains detailed scope and the bidders are expected to provide their bids based on the scope. In such a case, there are actually two projects. The first project is initiated by the customer to plan the scope and the second one is initiated by the construction company to plan the rest of the parts of the project (time, cost etc.) and to carry out the project. This is as shown in the diagram below:

Irrespective of the timing of the scope planning, it is important to know that scope planning needs to happen in its entirety. For the sake of simplicity we shall assume that the scope is being planned as part of the same project after receipt of the project charter so that we can include all the planning activities in the same project. The requirements gathering and scope planning stages described below will still apply to tender based industries with a difference that this would happen as part of two different projects.

Requirements Gathering

Once the project charter has been issued and stakeholders have been identified, the next thing to do is gathering of requirements. Requirements may be gathered either by visiting the customer premises, over emails, over phone, or various other means. This will obviously require project resources. How requirements would be gathered and using which template will all be defined in the project plan.

Requirements document is a very company specific artefact and, hence, would differ from company to company. Below is a template that can be used for capturing requirements. It can be tailored to the need of the company.

Req ID	Description	Type	Acceptance Criteria	Requester Information			Priority	Included	Phase
				Name	Role	Stake holder ID			

Given below is a description of the requirements document template shown above:

Req ID

Requirement identifier. Each requirement should have unique identifier.

Description

Description of the actual requirement

Type

Functional or Non-functional. Functional requirements are those given by the stakeholders that are related to the functionality that the product should have. Non-functional requirements are like performance parameters that do not provide any functionality but determine the usability of the product. For example, while developing a website, functional requirements would specify the functionality to be provided by each webpage. Non-functional requirements would state how fast each webpage should open, what is the availability percentage of the application etc.

Acceptance Criteria

These are objective and measurable criteria agreed upon with the stakeholder for each requirement. When these criteria are met we conclude that the requirement has been successfully delivered.

Requester Information

Information of the stakeholder who asked for the requirement. This is important so as to know who to go back to for clarification and sign-off.

Priority

The priority determines how important the requirement is. It can be Low, Medium, High or Need to have, Nice to have, Good to have etc. It gives an idea on which requirements are absolutely important and have to be delivered in the first phase in case the project is being done in phases as the entire project cannot be fit into the schedule.

Included

This field contains either Yes or No. Some requirements may not be agreed upon by the sponsor or are not feasible. These may still be documented here for future reference but excluded from the project scope.

Phase

Determines the phase in which a particular requirement will be delivered.

Below is a sample requirements document for a project to create a company's website. Please note that this is not a complete document but a part of it is shown here for understanding purpose.

Req ID	Description	Type	Acceptance Criteria	Requester Information			Priority	Included	Phase
				Name	Role	Stake holder ID			
1	The home page of the website would show a graphic of the company's vision and achievements	Functional	Home page opens in IE 6.0, Mozilla 11.0 showing the video	Cust1	Customer	1	High	Yes	1
2	The "About Us" page will allow users to browse company information	Functional	Company information opens in above browsers and shows names of directors, their background, company address and phone numbers	Cust2	Customer	2	High	Yes	1
3	The "Login" page will allow users to view additional information about the company	Functional	Users should be able to create their own login-id and password which are stored in the application so can login later on. Once logged-in users can view financial results of the company and it's product details	User1	End-User	5	Medium	Yes	2
4	Each webpage will open within 5 secs	Non-Functional	The home page of the website would show a graphic of the company's vision and achievements	User2	End-User	4	High	Yes	1

Creation of Scope Statement

Once the requirements have been collected and documented we need to finalize the scope. This is done using a scope statement.

This is generally in the form of a document and details out all the work that needs to be done on the project. This is again a company specific template but the one below can also be used with customizations, if any are required.

PROJECT SCOPE STATEMENT

Product Scope Description

<Detailed description of the characteristics of the product of the project>

Product Acceptance Criteria

<What are the measurable characteristics/tests that need to pass in order to accept the product of the project>

Project Deliverables

<Detailed list of the various things that the project will deliver>

Project Exclusions

<List of items not in the project scope for clarity purpose>

Project Constraints

<Detailed list of constraints that need to be kept in mind while managing the project>

<Will include schedule, cost, resources, technology, quality and other expectations that limit the project manager's options>

Project Assumptions

<All assumptions made during scope planning that need to be shared

with all stakeholders to get them on the same page and for their buy-in>
Below is a sample scope statement for the website development project:

PROJECT SCOPE STATEMENT

Product Description

The product of the project is a website that provides access to potential and existing customers. It gives company details, description of the company's products and services etc.

Project Deliverables

a) Website opening with the Home Page showing a video file

b) "About Us" page

c) Login functions – Create, login, logout, view/edit profile

d) Pages showing additional information about the company after login

Product Acceptance Criteria

a) All pages of the website should open without any error in IE 6.0 and Mozilla 11.0

b) Some pages that require login should only open after user logs in

c) Users should be able to manage their login online – creation, update

d) All pages should open within 5 seconds of clicking on the hyperlink for the page

e) The website should be able to support at least 100 concurrent users

f)   The website up time is guaranteed to be at least 99.9%. This will be verified over a 1 week period by giving it maximum

Project Exclusions

a)   This project will only provide the development of the new website

b)   Regular maintenance work of the website is not included in this scope

c)   No ongoing support would be provided within the scope of the project once the project has been signed-off

d)   All hardware and software procurements are out of scope of this project. They are to be provided separately by the customer on their premises

Project Assumptions and Constraints

a)   Customer will provide all required hardware and software licenses to develop and host the website.

b)   The project would use open source software, wherever possible, in order to keep the total development and operational cost low.

c)   No automated load testing would be performed. The customer agrees to provide several users for manual load testing.

Work Breakdown Structure

Once the scope has been finalized in the scope statement, it then needs to be well understood, estimated, allocated, and monitored by the project team. This can only be done by breaking it down into smaller, more manageable pieces of work. Such a process of decomposing scope creates a hierarchical structure called Work Breakdown Structure (WBS). Diagram below shows how a WBS looks.

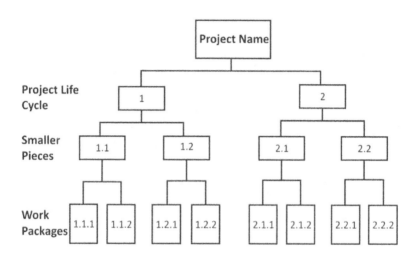

The WBS starts with the name of the project at its top level. The next level can either be the project life cycle/phases, deliverables, or sub-projects. This decomposition continues until a stage is reached when the work cannot be broken down any further or is small enough to estimate, allocate, and manage, or will be outsourced. We stop decomposing at this stage and call it a Work Package – the bottom-most level in a WBS. We also use a WBS Numbering system to uniquely identify each work package and the level at which it resides as each time we go one level down an additional dot is added to the numbering. An element at level two would look like 1.2, 2.3 etc. and the element at level four would look like 2.1.3.4, 3.4.2.1 etc. This numbering is very handy while reporting status on work packages. Below WBS shows the first few levels of a construction project.

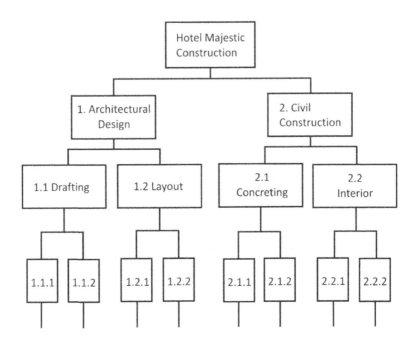

There is no one way of making a WBS. It is a very subjective area where very few people would come up with exactly the same WBS. However, there is one rule that determines if the WBS is correct. And, that is whether the WBS covers all the work needed to be done on the project. If it does then the WBS is correct because work not included in the WBS is out of scope of the project.

Below is a sample WBS for the earlier project on website development. This is not a complete WBS as it is not broken down to the work package level. Only the first two levels are shown here.

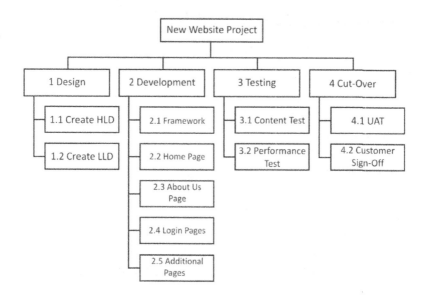

At the bottom-most level of the WBS we have work packages. A project would have several work packages and, hence, it might be difficult to remember the description of each work package for future reference. Hence, a one-page document is generally maintained in order to capture the description of each work package. This is called a WBS dictionary. It may contain anything the project manager wishes to document about each work package.

Below is a suggested template that could be used for a WBS dictionary.

WBS DICTIONARY

Work Package#	Date of Update	Responsible Organization/Person
Work Package Description		
Acceptance Criteria		
Deliverables		
Assumptions		
Resources		
Duration		
Planned Cost		
Schedule Start Date		Schedule Finish Date

At this point of time in the planning process we haven't decided on resources working on each work package, nor have we estimated the time and cost of each work package. Hence, the above WBS Dictionary would only be partially filled at this point of time and revisited later during the planning process to fill in the other details.

Time Planning

In scope planning we determine the work that needs to be delivered on the project. Next we need to know what activities/tasks need to executed, how much time each would take, in what sequence they would be carried out, and by how many resources. All these questions are answered in time planning.

Identification of Activities

A WBS ends with work packages. These are the smallest pieces of deliverables on a project. We start with the work packages and identify the tasks/activities that need to be performed in order to deliver the work packages. This means one more level of decomposition as shown below.

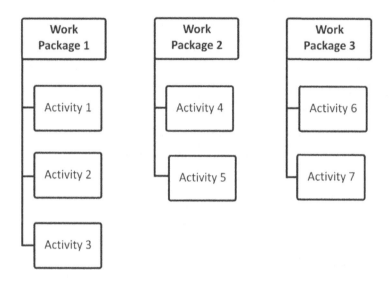

This gives us a list of activities that need to be performed on the project. Along with the activities we also need to document their details like we did for a work package in the WBS dictionary. This description is kept in Activity Attributes. These attributes contain all details that need to be documented for the activities for better understanding during execution.

Sequencing of Activities

Once the activities have been identified they need to be put in the sequence they should occur. Some are dependent while others are independent. This will give us an idea on which activity can happen first, what happens next, and what can happen in parallel.

Let's assume that we identify seven activities to be part of our project. These activities take care of the entire project scope. This would generally be rare as even simple projects would contain tens of activities but we consider only seven for simplicity sake. The seven activities are – 1 through 7. From our project understanding we realize that activities 1 and 4 are independent and can be started as soon as the project starts. Activity 2 depends on 1 and can only happen after 1 is completed. Activity 3 can only happen after activity 2 has completed. Similarly, activity 5 depends on 4, 6depends on 5 and 7 depends on 6. Using this information, we draw the below diagram showing this sequencing.

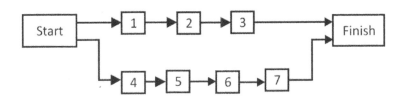

The diagram shown above is called a Network Diagram. It shows activity dependencies in a project. Each node (box) shows an activity and each arrow shows a dependency. The dependencies can be of three types:

a) **Mandatory dependency** – The dependency exists from the nature of work and there is no way to remove it. For example, manufacturing cannot begin without design completion.

b) **Discretionary dependency** – This dependency has been inserted as per the discretion of the project manager in order to reduce project risk. For example, getting government approvals may not always be mandatory to start building construction work but due to high risk involved the project manager might decide to wait until the approvals are in place.

c) **External dependency** – This is a dependency that the project has on an external party. For example, if a particular deliverable will be created and delivered by a vendor then those project activities that depend on this deliverable would have an external dependency.

Most common dependency is the one where an activity's start depends on another activity's finish. This is called Finish-to-Start dependency or, simply, F-S. There are three other possible ways to show a dependency as shown below:

a) **Finish-to-start (F-S)** – An activity cannot start until its predecessor has finished. For example, development of a software module can only start after the design has been completed.

b) **Start-to-start (S-S)** – An activity cannot start before the start of its predecessor activity. For example, testing of a software module cannot start before its development but once development starts it can happen in parallel and test whatever portion has been completed.

c) **Finish-to-finish (F-F)** – An activity cannot finish before the finish of its predecessor activity. For example, creation of a user manual of a product can happen in parallel with its development but cannot complete until the development has finished as there could be changes that need to be included in the manual.

d) **Start-to-finish (S-F)** – An activity cannot finish until its predecessor has started. This is a rarely used dependency. An example would be handover of 24x7 customer service from one person to another. Until the next person arrives (starts) the person from the previous shift cannot leave (finish). Below are the ways the above dependencies are shown in the network diagram:

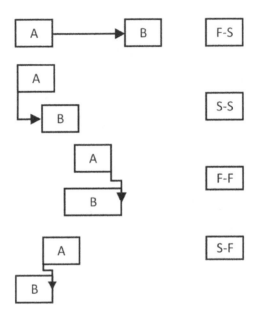

In a network diagram the most commonly used dependency is F-S. In this dependency, the successor activity can start as soon as the predecessor activity finishes. However, there are instances when we need to wait between the finish of the predecessor and start of the successor. This is called Lag. For example, if the predecessor activity is pouring concrete on a slab and the successor activity is to paint on the concrete slab, there will be a waiting time (lag) in between as concrete needs curing time so that it does not develop cracks. During this time no activity is performed on the slab.

There are times when we are able to start an activity a little ahead of its predecessor's finish by taking a little higher risk in an F-S dependency. This is called Lead and is exactly opposite of Lag. In fact, scheduling tools, like Microsoft Project, call it negative Lag. For example, for a software development project, we have a dependency that the coding would only start after the design has been completed and approved. However, in order to save some time, we often start coding a little early when we are sure that the design, although not approved, may not see major changes.

Estimating Duration of Activities

Once we have identified the activities and their sequences, in order to put calendar dates, we would need to know their durations. Activity duration depends on two things – effort and resources. Effort is the "man days" or "man hours" required to complete an activity. It is the amount of effort that needs to be put on an activity. After estimating the effort, the duration can be computed based on the number of resources working on the activity. For example, if the effort is 8 man hours then the duration would be 1 day if one resource works on the activity. It will be about 0.5 day if two resources work on it and so on. Below is the formula for calculating the duration:

Effort = Duration x Number of Resources

Or, stated in a different way,

Duration = Effort/Number of Resources

There are several ways of estimating the effort of an activity. Each of these is listed below.

Parametric Estimate

If an activity is about painting a room, then one of the most common estimates is to use a thumb rule of how much time it takes to paint one square foot of wall. Next, we take the total measurement of all the walls to be painted. We get the final estimate by multiplying the thumb rule with the total square feet. This is called a Parametric Estimate and is generally the most accurate because the thumb rule is made using data from past projects and expert judgement. Another example would be when trying to estimate the time taken to excavate (dig) for building construction. Thumb rule for excavating one cubic meter would be used and depending upon the total volume of the excavation the final figure can be arrived at. In software development projects we regularly use Function Point (FP) based estimation. In this technique we calculate the number of function points and use a standard productivity chart to arrive at the final "man days" estimate of activities. This is also a parametric estimate.

Parametric Estimate = Thumb Rule per unit x Number of units

One-time Estimate

There are times when the project manager asks the concerned team member or a subject matter expert to estimate the time required to do an activity. The team member would give a figure based on expert judgement and this estimate would generally contain a buffer. For example, if the project manager asks the team member to estimate the duration for painting a wall, based on the person's expertise he believes that the work can be completed in 5 days but would rather say 6 days just in case something goes wrong. This buffer is not known to the project manager. Hence, this kind of estimate could be filled with buffers for each activity and all buffers would add up to give a longer than actual schedule. This would also inflate the costs as they depend on the efforts. The situation is worse if there are multiple levels of hierarchy involved in time estimation. If in the above case the team leader asks the team member and gets an estimate of 5 days, he would probably report 6 days as estimate to the project manager as he is unaware of the buffer already been kept by the team member. These buffers add up to create a very inflated schedule. It is not a good project management practice to have buffers. Instead, there should be reserves at the end of the schedule. Reserves are known to everybody and kept for the entire project based on project risks.

PERT (Program Evaluation and Review Technique)

In the previous two estimation types, we used historical data from past projects and/or expert judgement to arrive at an estimate. This is only possible when such work has been performed in the past. However, if the activity is a totally new one or differs enough from the one done in the past, then we may not be able to come up with an accurate figure for the effort estimate. In such cases, we can use PERT. This technique suggests the use of three estimates – Optimistic (O), Most Likely (M) and Pessimistic (P).

An Optimistic estimate is the earliest possible completion of the activity

A Pessimistic estimate is the latest possible completion of the activity

A Most Likely estimate is the most probable completion of the activity

We then apply the PERT formula to calculate the PERT duration of the estimate. It is also called weighted average duration and is given by the formula below:

PERT Estimate = (O + 4M + P)/6

For example, if an activity has the following estimates:

O = 5 days

M = 8 days

P = 10 days

Then, PERT Estimate = (5 + (4x8) + 10)/6 = 47/6 = 7.833 days

As "Most Likely" has been given four times weight, the PERT estimate would be very close to it.

When using a PERT estimate, we are also interested to know how much risk is involved in the activity's estimate as that helps us determine the probability of completing the project on time. This is done by calculating the Standard Deviation of a PERT estimate. Formula for calculating standard deviation is give below:

Standard Deviation = (P – O)/6

In the above example, Standard Deviation = (10 – 5)/6 = 5/6 = 0.833

It means that the activity can be completed within 7.833 +/- 0.833 days or anywhere between 7 and 8.666 days.

We shall see in the next section how we can calculate the standard deviation of the project when we are using PERT estimates for all activities in the project.

Once we estimate the duration of each activity using one of the above mentioned techniques, we then estimate the number of resources working on each activity. This gives us the activity durations that would be used for scheduling. It must be noted that law of diminishing returns applies to the conversion of effort to duration. For example, if an activity can be completed in 1 day by 1 person, then its duration is 1 day, and effort is also 1 day. If we add one more person to the same activity, then the duration may not go down to 0.5 days. It will take a little longer than that. This is because there will be an overhead of communication between the two resources. Hence, one needs to use expert judgement when converting effort to duration as it may not be a simple arithmetic calculation.

Scheduling

Now that we have the activities, their dependencies and durations, it is possible to put calendar dates and find the project schedule.

Let's look at the network diagram we made earlier:

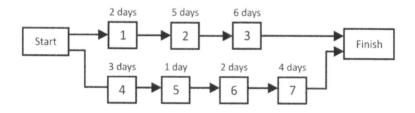

In the above diagram, we have now added the durations of each activity. This network diagram has two paths – 1-2-3 and 4-5-6-7. The first path takes 13 days and the second one takes 10 days to complete. It is obvious then that the project would take 13 days to complete as the second path of 10 days can be completed during this time. Hence, path 1-2-3 is called the "Critical Path" of the project. A critical path is the longest path in the project's network diagram that dictates how long a project would take. It also tells a project manager which activities are on the critical path, and hence, to spend more monitoring and controlling time on these activities. In the above diagram, the project manager's time is best spent on monitoring activities 1, 2 and 3 as any delay on these would delay the project.

Activities on the critical path cannot be delayed at all without delaying the project. Hence, they do not have any "float" or "slack", or the "float" or "slack" is zero. Similarly, activities on the other paths can be delayed by a certain amount without delaying the project. In the above diagram, activities 4, 5, 6 and 7 can be delayed by 3 days (13-10) without affecting the end date of the project. Hence, all these activities have a float or slack of 3 days. Although we talk of float per activity, it is actually the float of the entire path. It is the path 4-5-6-7 that can be delayed by up to 3 days and not each activity on the path.

Let's consider another network diagram like the one below:

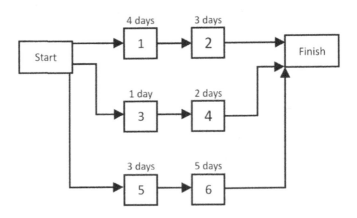

Here we have three paths in the network diagram. The critical path is 5-6 as it takes 8 days. The other two paths, 1-2 and 3-4 take 7 days and 3 days respectively. However, path 1-2 is very close to the critical path as it has a float of only 1 day. Such paths that are close to the critical path are each called Near Critical Path. These are those paths that have the capability of becoming the critical path in future if there is a slight delay in activities on such paths. The definition of a near critical path is very subjective and depends upon the project schedule and the project manager's risk taking ability. For longer projects a path that is 1 month away from the critical path could be near critical, whereas, for shorter projects a path that is 1 week away could be near critical. Some project managers are very risk averse and would like to call a path that is 15 days away as near critical, whereas, risk seeking project managers might call a path that is only 7 days away as near critical. Activities on near critical path are the project manager's next priority for monitoring as they have the ability of becoming critical path in future.

A project can have multiple critical paths but that would increase the risk on the project because the project manager now needs to worry about multiple paths that have the ability of delaying the project. Similarly, a project can also have multiple near critical paths.

Once we know the critical path of the project along with the project start date, it is possible to compute the project's end date and put start and end dates for each activity in the project. Below diagram shows how a Gantt Chart (Bar Chart) for the network diagram seen above looks. It shows the schedule of a project. The difference between a Gantt chart and a network diagram is that the bars in Gantt chart change in length based on the activity duration and we can also show progress using a Gantt chart (from Microsoft Project 2010®).

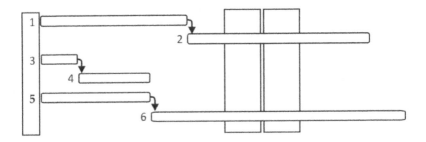

It would also be useful to know which activity should start at what time so that the project is not delayed. When it comes to the critical path there is no flexibility available as there is no float. But we have some flexibility on the other paths. Hence, we can get the early start and early finish dates for activities in these paths. Similarly, we can also get the late start and late finish dates for these activities. This tells us the window within which each of these activities needs to be started and finished to avoid a delay in the project.

In order to calculate the early start and finish we need to do a forward pass through the network diagram. We always start with the critical path and then take the other paths as shown below.

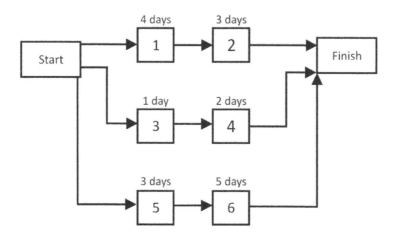

The critical path is 5-6. We start putting days against these in the forward pass. Start from activity 5. It can start immediately as the project start, on day 0. It takes 3 days so finishes by day 3. Activity 6 starts immediately on day 3 and finishes on day 8, as it takes 5 days. Similarly, we put the early start and finish dates for other paths as well as shown in the diagram. This tells us that activity 2 can start no earlier than day 4.

Next, we do a backward pass through the network diagram and find the late start and finish dates for each activity. Start with critical path and then take the other paths.

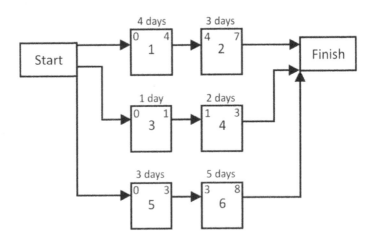

Starting with the critical path, 5-6, and coming from finish to start, we understand that activity 6 needs to complete latest by day 8 to complete the project on time. In such a case it needs to start by day 3, as activity 5 needs to finish by day 3 and needs to start on day 0. The late start and finish dates for activity 5 and 6 are same as their early start and finish dates as these activities are on the critical path.

Next, take path 1-2 from finish to start. Activity 2 can be finished by day 8 and the project can still be on schedule. Then it needs to start by day 5 as it takes 3 days. Activity 1 needs to complete by day 5 and should start by day 1 as it takes 4 days. Similarly, we also calculate the late start and finish dates for activities 3 and 4. What this analysis tells us is that activity 2 needs to start between day 4 and day 5 in order for the project to complete on time. Similarly, activity 4 needs to finish between days 3 and 8 for the project to be on time. The difference between the late start and early start or between late finish and early finish is also the float of the activity.

Float = LS – ES or LF – EF

There are other ways of showing a schedule, like using a milestone chart. A milestone is a date by when a set of activities complete. For example, for a construction project, there could be a milestone for completion of 1st floor of the building, another for construction of 2nd floor etc. A milestone chart shows only the milestones against a timeline instead of detailed tasks. This information is especially important when showing status to senior management or to the finance team of the company as payments are generally linked to milestones. Below diagram shows a milestone chart (in Microsoft Project 2010®).

04 Jun '12							11 Jun '12						
M	T	W	T	F	S	S	M	T	W	T	F	S	S

◇ 04 - 06

◇ 11 - 06

It shows two milestones that would be achieved in 4th June and 11th June. These dates depend upon the tasks that need to be performed to achieve the milestones.

If we are using PERT for calculating the duration of every activity then we can also calculate the standard deviation of the project. Assume that the activities below depict critical path activities.

Activity	PERT Duration	Standard Deviation	Variance
1	10	1	1
2	4	0.5	0.25
3	8	1.5	2.25
Total	22	-	3.50

The variance is calculated by taking a square of the standard deviation using the below formula:

Variance = (Standard Deviation) x (Standard Deviation)

If we need to know the standard deviation of the entire project, then we need to add all the variances and takes a square root as below:

Total Variance = 1 + 0.25 + 2.25 = 3.5 days

Standard Deviation = (Variance) ^ 0.5 = 1.87 days

Hence, we say that the project will complete within 22 +/- 1.87 days

Schedule Compression

If the developed schedule does not fit within the expected timelines, then we need to compress the schedule. There are two primary ways of doing this.

Crashing

One way to compress the schedule is by increasing the resources on the critical path activities. These resources can either be picked up from the non-critical activities or new hires from outside the project. This action generally increases the project cost and is called Crashing.

Fast Tracking

If there is a possibility of removing some discretionary

dependencies and doing some activities in parallel it is called Fast Tracking. This comes with higher risk on the project as there is a possibility of rework because some dependencies have been removed.

Finally, if the project manager is unable to compress the schedule enough using the above two techniques then the project could be delivered in phases. This will require some negotiation between the stakeholders and the high priority requirements included in Phase 1. The next phases would include the rest of the requirements.

Cost Planning

Once the project's schedule has been created, we set out to determine the detailed budget for the project. Although the Project Charter provides the project budget, it is a ballpark figure that is expected to have a certain percentage of variance. At this stage we do detailed estimation of all the project costs and determine whether this budget fits within the one mentioned in the project charter or not. If it does not fit then we either need to increase the budget mentioned in the project charter or drop some scope.

Estimating Cost of Activities

The first step towards creating a project budget is by estimating costs associated with each activity. There can be fixed and variable costs. We generally estimate only the direct costs associated with the project activities. The indirect costs are then added while budgeting, but these costs are not in control of the project manager and would be incurred irrespective of the project as they are overheads.

An activity is taken and all costs for it are estimated. If any equipment is bought for it or if any setup costs, are involved then these will be the fixed costs for the activity. Any use of materials or human resources would generally entail variable costs. All these costs are then added to get the total costs for the activity. The below format could be used for doing this calculation:

Activity	Fixed Costs(F)	Variable Costs (V)			Activity Cost (F+V)
		Resource Cost Per Day/Cost Per Item(A)	Number of Days/Number of Items(B)	Total Variable Cost(A×B)	
1	$100	$400	20	$800	$900

The methods used to estimate effort for activities are Parametric, One-time, and PERT. The same methods can also be used to estimate the cost of activities in terms of $.

Budgeting

Coming up with a project budget is a simple addition of all the individual activity estimates. However, there are also some additional items that need to be added to get to the final budget. These are two levels of reserves – contingency reserve and management reserve. Contingency reserve is kept for known risks on the project. For example, if one of the risks on the project is related to thefts then there will be some money kept aside to take care of the damage in case this risk happens. Management reserve is for unknown risks. There are several things that the project manager may not envision on the project. So, if they do happen, then some money needs to be kept aside to handle the damage. This is done by the management reserve.

First, we add up all the individual activity costs to come up with the total direct costs on the project. Then we add the indirect costs. Companies generally estimate indirect costs by using a certain percentage of the direct costs. After adding the indirect costs to the direct costs, we get the total project cost. It may be noted that sometimes companies use a per hour or per day resource cost that includes both direct and indirect costs. In such cases we do not need to add indirect costs separately. Then the sum of all activity costs would be the project costs.

Contingency reserve is the first reserve added to the project costs. It is also a percentage and depends on two things – riskiness of the project and the policy of the company. Companies generally use a fixed percentage for contingency reserve for an average risk project for the company. For projects with lesser or higher risks, the percentage would be lower or higher respectively. After addition of this reserve we get the project baseline. A project manager manages the project against this number and the actual numbers are compared against this. If the project stays within the baseline, then it is considered to be successful.

Management reserve is the last reserve to be added and is used as a fixed percentage of the project baseline. This percentage is fixed by the company for all projects in the company. This gives us the project budget. The entire calculation is shown in graphical form below:

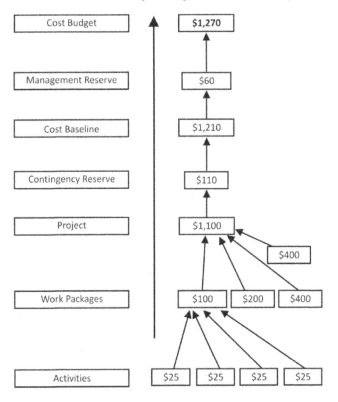

In the above example we have assumed that the indirect costs are included in the individual activity costs, so they are not added separately.

The sheet below shows the template that can be used for calculating the project budget. It contains separate indirect costs.

The project manager is not allowed to utilize the management reserve. Only when unknown risks occur permission may be granted for its utilization.

Activity	Fixed Costs (F)	Variable Costs(V)			Total Cost (F+V)
		Resource Cost Per Day/Cost Per Item (A)	Number of Days/ Number of Item (B)	Total Variable Costs (A×B)	
1	$1,000	$100	10	$1,000	$2,000
2	-	$400	15	$6,000	$6,000
3	-	$250	10	$2,500	$2,500
4	$20,00	-	20	-	$20,000
Total Direct Costs					$30,500
Indirect Costs(10% of Direct Costs)					$3,050
Project Costs(Direct + Indirect Costs)					$33,550
Contingency Reserve(10% of Project Costs)					$3,355
Cost Baseline(Project Costs + Contingency Reserve)					$36,905
Management Reserve(2% of Cost Baseline)					$3,690
Cost Budget(Cost Baseline + Management Reserve)					$40,595

Quality Planning

Quality is a term which is very often misunderstood in projects. It is several times equated to adhering to quality standards or providing the best possible features to a product. In reality, Quality is about meeting requirements. The requirements come from stakeholders of the project and are base lined in the scope statement seen earlier. As long as the project meets these, we say that quality has been achieved. Trying to deliver more than this would mean over delivering and is referred to as "Gold Plating". The project does not get paid for delivering extra and ends up reducing the profitability of the project, although it may increase customer satisfaction. But this benefit is generally short lived as the customer will expect more extras in the future deliveries which would mean further reduction of profitability of projects. Hence, it is better to deliver what has been asked for and nothing more and, obviously, nothing less.

Metrics

In order to achieve the desired quality, we plan quality activities, like reviews, inspections and testing. Outputs of these are called metrics, or measurements. These metrics are compared against the range that is acceptable on the project. For example, for a construction project, one of the metrics used is strength of concrete. The concrete is sent for strength test to see how much pressure it can withstand before it breaks down. If that is within the acceptable range decided for the project, then we say that the quality check has passed. Similarly, for software project, there are metrics related to number of defects found while carrying out testing. If the percentage of defects are within an acceptable range (say, <5%), then the software application is allowed to go to the next stage. If the project procures some materials from suppliers, then specific quality checks are decided for them and the lot is accepted only if it satisfies these.

While deciding the appropriate metrics to be used on the project we look at similar projects in the past, use company's guidelines, and do benchmarking by looking at the best companies in the industry. This gives us a list of metrics to be used along with their acceptable range.

Cost of Quality

Quality is more to do about prevention than inspection. This is because if something has been made with better quality then little effort and money needs to be spent in inspecting it. On the other hand, if things are being done without much regards to quality and there is a heavy dependency on inspection then the project spends too much on rework. It is also best to have in-process inspection at various points within the process while the product is being produced instead of final inspection. If a defect is caught early, it takes less time and money to fix it. This concept has been very well explained by W. Edwards Deming as Cost of Quality (CoQ). Quality has costs of conformance and costs of non-conformance. Cost of conformance are all those costs that are expended in trying to achieve good quality. Cost of non-conformance are all those costs that are expended because the quality is not good. Below are the components of both:

Cost of Conformance	Cost of Non-conformance
Process improvement	Rework
Quality training	Scrap
Inspection	Loss of business due to adverse impact on brand image
Testing	Warranty/liability costs
	Litigation costs

CoQ = Cost of Conformance + Cost of Non-conformance

When we invest $1 in the cost of conformance, we tend to save >$1 from the cost of non-conformance, thereby reducing the CoQ. This continues until we reach the optimum level of quality. After this, additional $1 in cost of conformance gives <$1 savings in cost of non-conformance. We always plan to achieve this optimum level of quality.

Human Resource Planning

Every project needs resources. These can be human resources, machines and materials. Human resources are probably the only resources used in services. Hence, a project needs to plan human resources that would be required. This would include the numbers of resources, their locations, and their skills.

Organisational Structure

Every company has a structure in which it is organized. Similarly, every project also has a structure. This can be depicted in two ways –using reporting relationship and using skills. When we create a structure showing reporting relationships it is called Organisational Breakdown Structure (OBS) as shown below:

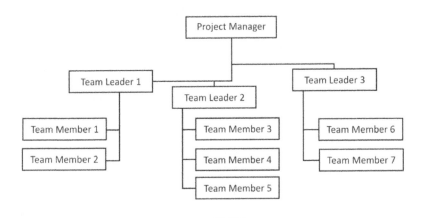

When the structure is made on the basis of skills of the team it is called Resource Breakdown Structure (RBS) as shown below:

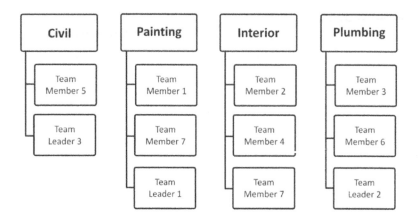

It might sometimes be more convenient to combine both the structures, OBS and RBS, to show both reporting relationships and skills at once as shown below:

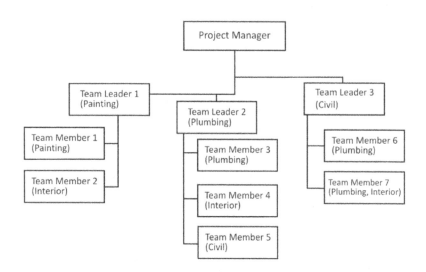

Responsibility Assignments

The activities identified earlier in time planning have to be assigned to specific resources. These work assignments are documented in a Responsibility Assignment Matrix (RAM) or RACI Matrix. Below is an example of a RAM shown for 4 project activities:

Activity	John	Mary	Leon	Jack
1	R	A	C	I
2		R,A		C,I
3	R	C	R,A	I
4		C	I	R,A

In the above matrix, R stands for "Responsible", A stands for "Accountable", C is "Consult", and I is "Inform". R is put against the person(s) who would be performing the activity. Activity 1 is going to be done by John, 2 by Mary and so on. There could be multiple persons responsible for an activity so we may have multiple R's like for activity 3. A is put against the person who is accountable for the work performed on an activity. There should be one and only one person accountable for each activity. Ideally responsibility and accountability should go together unless there is a junior team member, like John, for whom Mary takes accountability as John reports to Mary. C is used to denote the person who can be consulted in case of any queries and is optional. I is used to denote the person who should be informed about the status of the activity, probably because that person's activity depends on the completion of this activity. This is also optional.

When there are several team members it might be difficult to make a RAM/RACI Matrix like the one shown above. In such case we may use the one shown below:

Activity	Responsible	Accountable	Consult	Inform
1	John	Mary	Leon	Jack
2	Mary	Mary	Jack	Jack
3	Jack, Leon	Leon	Mary	Jack
4	Jack	Jack	Mary	Leon

Staffing Decisions

Once we have done the work assignment, we would be able to come up with staffing requirements in the form of a Resource Histogram. It is a bar chart showing staff requirements over the period of the project as shown below:

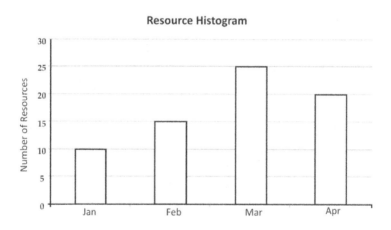

The plan should also include ways of hiring and releasing resources. Project resources can either be hired from within the company or from outside by recruiting new resources.

If there are any project specific skills required then we also need to identify training needs for the project. Although we may not be able to decide the exact training dates, we should at least identify the month/quarter when the training would be conducted and how many resources would need to attend it. Finally, every project should have a Rewards and Recognition (R&R) system. This will inherit the company's reward and recognition policies but the project manager should mention the objective criteria on how the team members can get these. This is very important in keeping the team motivated.

Communications Planning

Every project needs to communicate with its stakeholders. Details of the communication are to be decided for each project during planning and documented. They should contain the following:

a) **Who will communicate**

Project's performance reports should be communicated by a pre-designated person or set of persons. This ensures that there is no redundancy or mismatch between different communications.

b) **What will be communicated**

It is important that the performance report formats and frequencies are agreed upon with the stakeholders. The project team would generally suggest the details that they would send in the reports and get an agreement with the stakeholders. Stakeholders have different communication requirements. Some would like to get detailed reports, whereas, others would like to get summary reports. Similarly, they would also need reports at different frequencies.

c) **When will the communication happen**

Every project sends reports at a set frequency – daily, twice a week, weekly, fortnightly, monthly etc. Many stakeholders would like to get a frequent report, say weekly and, another less frequent report, say monthly. All this needs to be captured and documented.

d) **How will it be communicated**

There are various communication mediums using which reports can be sent. Most common mediums are letter, fax, and email. Stakeholders would have their own choice of medium using which they should receive the reports.

Communication Model

Communication happens between two people, sender and receiver. In order for the communication to be effective there are certain pre-requisites. Effective communication means that the message sent by the sender has been understood by the receiver. Diagram below shows the communication model:

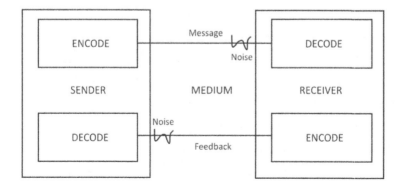

It is the responsibility of the sender to correctly encode the message being sent to the receiver. Encoding could mean different things for different types of communications. For verbal communication, it is the language, pronunciation, and the speed of the speech. For written communication, it is the language, spelling, and the handwriting. A very important aspect of encoding is also to understand the level of understanding of the receiver before sending communication. For example, some receivers could be experts and the sender can use highly technical words while communicating with them. But some receivers could be laymen and the sender should not be using too many technical words while communicating with them or else they may not understand. In summary, the sender needs to come to the level of understanding of the receiver for communicating.

It is also important for the sender to use the correct communication medium. For all contractual communication the communication has to be written, negotiations are best done face-to-face, whereas, performance reports are best sent either as hard copies or through email attachments.

The sender should ask the receiver to acknowledge that the message has been understood. When we talk over the phone in a noisy area we do ask the other party if they understood the message. In email communication we often add a line like "Please let me know if you have any queries or concerns". It becomes the responsibility of the receiver to provide feedback that the message has been understood. This completes the feedback loop and the communication is said to be effective.

There are also several noises that could interfere with the communication. These can be physical in nature, like background noise of traffic. They can also be related to mind blocks, like closed nature of a person, prejudices etc. The sender and receiver need to be aware of these noises and ensure that the communication is effective even in the presence of the noise.

Risk Planning

There are several uncertainties present while executing projects. These give rise to risks on projects. Risks are those uncertainties that have some impact on the outcome of the project. If something is known for sure there is no uncertainty, and, hence, no risk. Risk exists only for those events that have a probability of occurrence anywhere between 0 and100 percent. This means that the event may or may not occur.

Risks may be negative ones that cause harm to the project (called threats) or positive ones that cause benefit to the project (called opportunities). We are most often worried about the threats as they have the ability of derailing the project.

Inadequate risk planning is the top cause of project failures. Risks are often handled on an ad-hoc basis as they happen rather than being thought of during planning. Such an approach is a recipe for disaster on projects. Risk management is more to do with planning than with monitoring of projects. It involves three phases – risk identification, analysis, and response.

Identification of Risks

The first, and the most important, step in risk management planning is to identify all the project risks. The most common ways of identifying risks on a project are brainstorming, historical information, and checklists. During a brainstorming session, the project manager asks team members to give their views on project risks. It is important that all ideas are written down without any analysis or opposition. This will motivate all participants to give their inputs without the fear of being rejected. Past projects are also a great means of providing risks as they were actually encountered on similar projects and have a chance of being seen on this project as well. Companies often maintain a checklist of areas where risks are generally found. The checklist does not give actual risks but instead points to areas where risks are generally found. For example, the items in the checklist could be like technology complexity, weather conditions, employee capability etc. These provide inputs for the project manager to think of those areas in search for risks.

All the identified risks are inserted in a risk register. There is no limit to how many risks should be put in the risk register. It should contain as many risks as possible. Below is a template for risk register at this point:

Risk Id	Risk Statement	Category	Root Cause

Every risk should be given a unique number to identify it in. the form of a risk id. Risk statement is the actual detailed description of what the risk is. Risks are often categorized to know which area has more risks. Categories can be defined at a company level and customized at a project level and could have categories like, technical, financial, human resource etc. Root cause for each risk if identified can help in arriving at action plan for its resolution later on.

Analysis of Risks

The next stage is to analyze risks in order to prioritize them. This helps us know the top risks of the project on which we need to concentrate more. Some of the low risks may be knowingly ignored once the analysis is done. Analysis is performed on two basis – probability and impact. Probability is the chance of the risk happening and impact is the damage it can cause to the project. Either a qualitative scale of Low, Medium, High can be used for assessing both probability and impact, or a quantitative scale of 10%, 30%, 65% etc. can be used for the assessment. Companies have a policy of using either one of these for standardization and issue guidelines on how to use these scales. This data extends the risk register as below:

Risk Id	Risk Statement	Category	Root Cause	Probability	Impact	Severity	Priority

Severity is just the combination of probability and impact. Based on this combination the priority is decided.

Below is an example of a risk register with some analyzed risks:

Risk ID	Risk Statement	Category	Root Cause	Probability	Impact	Severity	Priority
1	Employee attrition during project execution	HR	Lower staff morale due to overtime work and rework. Lack of motivation due to few incentives.	M	M	MM	3
2	Unavailability of skilled resources during execution	HR	Special skills required on the project	H	H	HH	1
3	Delayed arrival of servers required for project integration	Procurement	Past records show that the servers are complex to build and require parts to be procured	M	H	MH	2
4	Delayed sign-off of project deliverables by customer leading to project delay	External	Customer involvement too low	L	M	LM	4

Responding to Risks

Once the risks have been prioritized we need to do something about them so they do not interfere with the project objectives. We start with the top priority risk and go down. The responses could be four – avoid, mitigate, transfer, accept.

Avoiding a risk means that taking action such that the risk has been completely removed. This is generally difficult to do and hence few risks are avoided. For example, if we decide to change the site of operations because the current site does not have necessary clearances, then we are avoiding the risk if the new site already has those clearances. Most common response to risks is mitigation. Mitigation means reduction in probability of the risk or impact of risk or both at once. Transfer of risk is done when our action transfers the risk to a third party. Most common ways of transferring are outsourcing and insurance. However, not all risks are transferrable. Finally, if nothing can be done about a risk or a risk is too low in priority we may decide to accept the consequences of the risk. This is an accept response. The risk register now looks as shown below:

Risk Id	Risk Statement	Category	Root Cause	Probability	Impact	Severity	Priority	Response

Below is the extension of the earlier risk register with appropriate responses:

Risk ID	Risk statement	Category	Root Cause	Probability	Impact	Severity	Priority	Response
1	Employee attrition during project execution	HR	Lower staff morale due to overtime work and rework. Lack of motivation due to few incentives.	M	M	MM	3	Mitigate- keep enough contingency in schedule. Provide incentive for early delivery.
2	Unavailability of skilled resources during execution	HR	Special skills required on the project	H	H	HH	1	Mitigate- keep list of probable candidates ready. Employ hiring agencies.
3	Delayed arrival of servers required for project integration	Procurement	Past records show that the servers are complex to build and require parts to be procured	M	H	MH	2	Mitigate & Transfer- Plan for vendor site visit once a week. Put late delivery penalty in vendor contract.
4	Delayed sign-off of project deliverables by customer leading to project delay	External	Customer involvement too low	L	M	LM	4	Accept

Procurement Planning

Projects either make things on their own or buy from outside. All buying is called procurement. In such a case, the project is the buyer and the vendor is the seller. A decision is first made on what to procure and what to make. After that, the project decides on how the procurement should happen – using which kind of contract.

Make-or-buy Decision

Projects have to do make-or-buy decisions in order to come up with a list of things that need to be procured. These decisions are based on several parameters. Most common parameters in favour of making are the following:

a) Project has expertise/capability in making it

b) Project has idle resources/free capacity

c) There is proprietary information involved in doing the work

d) It is cheaper to make

e) It is faster to make

f) It is not available in the market to buy

The common reasons for buying would be as follows:

a) Project does not have the capability to make it

b) Project does not have the capacity to make it

c) It is cheaper to buy

d) It is faster to buy (available off the shelf)

The make-or-buy decision gives a list of things that are to be procured. This list is taken through the rest of the procurement process.

Contract Type Selection

Once it has been decided what needs to be procured, we need to decide on the type of contract to be used. This decision is based on two factors – scope clarity and risk sharing. There are three types of contracts that can be used based on these two factors.

Cost Plus/Cost Reimbursable Contract

A Cost Plus contract has got two components – actual cost incurred by the vendor and the profit to be paid by the buyer. The buyer agrees to pay the seller at actual plus an additional profit for his services. The profit is pre-determined and can either be fixed or based on the cost. Below are the different ways of having a Cost Plus contract:

Cost + $10,000 per month as profit

Cost + 10% of Cost as profit

Cost + $2,000 per resource per month as profit

In this contract the buyer reimburses the actual costs of the seller and takes on almost all the risk of getting the work done. The seller is not concerned with the kind of work being done by the buyer so scope clarity is not required.

The invoices raised by the seller in this type of contract are detailed and mention the names of resources along with details of what work was carried out. The buyer needs to audit them to ensure that the seller is not trying to bill the buyer for work not carried out for them. If the buyer does not have resources to audit seller's invoices then this type of contract may not be preferable.

Rate Contract (Annual Rate Contract/Time and Material Contract)

In a Cost Plus contract the cost and profit are stated as separate components. In a Rate contract both are included in a single price. The buyer would not be aware of the seller's profit margin. Rates are agreed based on man hour, man day, per foot of steel, per cubic feet of concrete etc. These rates are generally negotiated once every year and a rate card is issued. Hence, it is also referred to as Annual Rate contract. Below are examples of a Rate contract:

$50 per hour for a Software Developer

$100 per hour for a Project Manager

$160 per day for an Electrician

Invoices are not as detailed as in a Cost Plus contract but still contain names of resources and their usage in hours, days etc. Below is an example of how the invoice looks:

Sr. No.	Name	Role	Rate (per day)	Consumption (days)	Total
1	Jack	Developer	$350	15	$5,250
2	Bob	Manager	$650	10	$6,500
3	HP Server	-	$1000	2	$2,000
			Total		$13,750

Fixed Price (FP)/Lumpsum Contract

A Lumpsum contract is signed between a buyer and a seller only based on clear scope. They decide a fixed price and other delivery terms, like date of delivery, expected quality, and location and mode of delivery. If the seller delivers the work meeting these delivery terms then the buyer pays the lumpsum amount.

However, if the seller fails to deliver then these contracts generally include penalty clauses that could reduce the seller's profit margin. If there are any cost overruns, the seller would have to incur them. Hence, most of the cost risk is passed on to the seller. The seller need not provide details of the number of resources being used or the details of their capacity utilization. Below is a quote for a Lumpsum contract:

Bid Price: $550,000 for delivery in 6 months

Bid Price: $750,000 for delivery in 4.5 months

The invoice in a Lumpsum contract is very short and only contains a single line about the delivery made against the contract as shown below:

Sr. No	Item Description	Amount
1	Web portal application-Release 1.0	$550,000
	Total	$550,000

These types of contracts may also include incentives that are payable when the performance is better than the one defined in the contract. The performance can be based on various parameters, like early delivery and better quality.

When a Lumpsum contract is signed for a longer term, like several years, it could be risky for the seller if the price of each item has been fixed based on the current price. If the price of an item rises, then under such a contract the increase in price would have to be borne by the seller. Hence, a Lumpsum contract also has a provision for an "escalation clause" that states that the price of the contract would go up (or even down) based on the price of certain commodities, or a market index. For example, if the contract involves buying a lot of cement for construction, the escalation clause may be linked to the market price of cement or the commodity market index. The contract states the price of cement that has been assumed while providing the lumpsum amount and any movement in the price would have proportional impact on the lumpsum amount.

Below table shows the best contract to use in different situations:

Scope Clarity	Risk Sharing	Contract Type to use
Low	Mostly with Buyer	Cost Plus
Medium	Shared between Buyer and Seller	Rate Contract
High	Mostly with Seller	Lumpsum

Approval and Kickoff Meeting

Once the project has been completely planned, the project plan is approved by the key stakeholders. This is when a Kickoff meeting is held. This meeting is not for reviewing the plan. The plan has already been approved. This meeting is to open communication channels between all stakeholders. Some of the discussions that happen during such a meeting are key project resource introductions, walkthrough of performance reports that would be sent and review of upcoming risks. Immediately after this meeting the project execution work is started.

Solved Examples

3.1 What is the significance of Project Scope Statement? Can a project be planned without a WBS?

Solution:

The Project Scope Statement gives a common understanding to all the stakeholders about what goes into the project. It is an important part of the scope baseline and determines what scope needs to be completed in order to call the project successful.

A WBS is created so that the project can be broken into smaller, more manageable pieces. Without it the project cannot be realistically estimated, work allocated or tracked. A WBS is not merely a diagram, but an agreement within the team that it consists of all the work and only the work needed to achieve the project scope statement.

3.2 Which of the following is the most accurate estimation technique?

   a) **One-time**

   b) **Parametric**

   c) **Analogous**

   d) **PERT**

Solution:

Parametric. This is because a parametric estimate is based on a thumb rule generated through past experience and expertise and is considered to be the most accurate measure.

3.3 Find the critical path in the below network diagram. What is float of activity D?

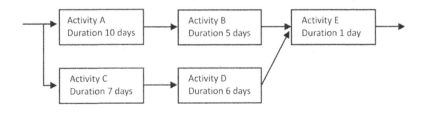

Solution:

The network diagram has the following paths:

A-B-E

C-D

Total duration of each path is:

A-B-E=16 days

C-D=14 days

Hence, A-B-E is the Critical Path

Activity D is on the non-critical path. Hence, its float is the difference between the duration of path C-D and the critical path, 16-14 = 2 days.

3.4 What is the purpose of Contingency Reserve?

a) Buffer for safety

b) Taking care of scope creep

c) Handling known risks on the project

d) Only used on large projects to take care of overruns

Solution:

Handling known risks on the project

3.5 "Quality should be more about prevention than inspection". Describe reasons for this statement.

Solution:

Quality on a project can be achieved using two means – taking preventive actions and taking corrective actions. When costs are incurred in order to improve the process used or in training personnel in quality, the project quality improves. This is called cost of prevention and it reduces cost of rework. When costs are incurred in inspecting or testing partly or fully finished products it is called cost of inspection. If defects are found then corrective action is implemented which leads to rework that will add effort and costs to the project. The later the defect is found the more costly it is to fix. Hence, a project is better off spending more in prevention costs than in inspection costs as it leads to better quality at a lesser cost.

3.6 A resource histogram shows what that a RACI matrix does not?

a) Time

b) Assignments

c) Resources

d) Dependencies

Solution:

Time

3.7 What needs to be defined in the communications planning stage of a project?

Solution:

During the communications planning stage we need to decide four parts related to project communications – who, what, when, and how. This should satisfy the needs of the stakeholders. It is part of project's stakeholder management strategy that could be different for different group of stakeholders or even individual stakeholders.

3.8 What is a Risk? Why should it be managed?

Solution:

Risk comes out of an uncertainty. Something that has a probability of occurrence greater than 0% and less than 100% and has some impact on the project is a project risk.

Negative risks (threats) have the ability of derailing projects. If not managed properly they could be the top reason for project failure. Hence, they need to be managed, more during planning stage.

3.9 Which of the following contracts is best to use when the scope is clear and the buyer wants to shift some risks?

a) Cost Plus

b) Rate Contract

c) Fixed Price

d) Incentivised contract

Solution:

Fixed Price

Practice Exercise

3.1 What is the need of a WBS Dictionary? What goes in it?

3.2 Why is Acceptance Criteria included in the Scope Statement?

3.3 What is the Critical Path in the below Network Diagram? Find float of all activities.

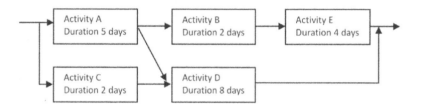

3.4 What is Quality? Who is responsible for it?

3.5 Which of the following shows reporting relationships?

a) Resource Histogram

b) Organisational Breakdown Structure

c) Resource Breakdown Structure

d) Network Diagram

3.6 Describe the meaning of Effective Communication. What is required for it to happen?

3.7 On what basis are risks analyzed? What is the purpose of this analysis?

3.8 Give some examples of how a rate card used in Rate contract would look. How often should it be updated?

Solutions to the above questions can be downloaded from the **Online Resources** *section of this book on* **www.vibrantpublishers.com**

Chapter Summary

◆ Planning on a project starts after the project has been initiated by a Project Charter.

◆ Scope Planning involves collecting and documenting requirements in a Requirements Document, defining project scope in a Project Scope Statement, and breaking down the scope into a Work Breakdown Structure (WBS). A WBS Dictionary provides description of elements in the WBS.

◆ Time Planning starts with activity identification, their sequencing, duration estimation, and schedule creation. A Parametric Estimate is the most accurate estimate. PERT (Program Evaluation and Review Technique) Estimate is used when there is a lot of uncertainty. A Schedule can be in the form of a Network Diagram or a Gantt/Bar Chart. The longest path in the project schedule is called the Critical Path of the project. Float or Slack means the amount of time that an activity can be delayed without delaying the project finish. Schedule Compression happens using Crashing or Fast Tracking. Crashing employs more resources, and Fast Tracking makes more activities parallel.

◆ Cost Planning involves estimation of activity level fixed and variable costs. Budgeting adds all these costs to get total project costs, to which contingency and management reserves are added to get the project budget.

◆ We then plan the quality parameters that will be

adhered to and tracked on the project. These are called metrics. While planning quality, we should consider all costs – costs of conformance and costs of non-conformance – cost of quality.

◆ Human Resource Planning includes creation of Organizational Breakdown Structure (OBS) to show the reporting relationship and Resource Breakdown Structure (RBS) to show the skill-wise breakdown of resources. A RACI Matrix provides data on activity level responsibilities. A Resource Histogram is created to show staff needs over time.

◆ While planning Communications, one must keep the communications model in mind and ensure that the sender encodes the messages being sent correctly, uses the correct medium for communication, asks for feedback from receiver, and the receiver provides the feedback. Communications Planning includes deciding and documenting who will be part of which project communications, along with the communication contents and timings.

◆ Risk Planning on projects is critical, as risks are the top reason for failure of projects. This involves risk identification, analysis, and responding to risks. Types of responses are – avoid, mitigate, transfer, and accept. Risks are placed in the risk register.

◆ In Procurement Planning, we do a make-or-buy analysis to decide what to procure from outside. We also make a contract type selection for each procurement. A Cost Reimbursable (CR) is contract is used for procurement when scope is not very clear and the buyer is willing to keep the risks. A Time & Material (T&M) contract is used when clarity of work is better and the risks are to be shared by both the parties of the contract. When the scope is very clear and the risks are to be passed on to the seller, a Fixed Price (FP) or Lumpsum contract is the most appropriate.

◆ Once the planning is done, the entire Project Management Plan is approved by the key stakeholders, and a kick-off meeting is held to formally open the communication channels between the stakeholders.

This page is intentionally left blank

Chapter **4**

Project Execution

The project execution starts once the plan is approved and kickoff meeting is completed. The aim of this stage is to mobilize the resources to perform the work mentioned in the plan.

Resource Mobilisation

Projects require resources – includes human resources and machines. The project plan states how many resources of what type are required at different times (resource histogram). Some projects work in multiple locations and, hence, have virtual teams (teams spread across geographies are called virtual teams). All these factors need to be kept in mind while mobilizing the right number of resources possessing the right skills at the right location.

This is a continuous process as resources are only hired when they are needed on the project. Holding resources would be a cost on the project hence projects hold on to them only for the required duration. In some cases they may be hired early if there is a risk of not getting them when needed. At other times some resources might be held on the project without much work if there are peaks and valleys in their usage. All these factors are already factored in the project cost budget. Any deviation from the resource acquisition plan could change the project cost.

Perform Project Execution

This is the main process of executing the project plan. Most of the project's time and cost is spent here. Resources perform the work as planned and produce deliverables. Data related to the effort spent on the deliverable, start and finish dates, and cost incurred, are also collected. This data is used to measure project variances for tracking the project against its baseline. Below is an example of the data collected for a particular activity:

Activity – ABC

Actual Effort	Actual Start	Actual Finish	Actual Cost
10 man days	1st June 2012	8th June 2012	$10,000

While a project is being executed changes might be identified to the plan. These would be originated by the person performing an activity. He may realize that the work cannot be performed as planned or there is a better way to do it. These are raised as Change Requests and go for approval. Approvals for those changes that have no impact or minimal impact on the schedule and cost may be approved by the project manager. Others might need approval from key stakeholders. The authority level would be mentioned in the project charter and reiterated in the project plan.

Team Management

While the project is being executed the project manager needs to develop and manage the team members. There are various aspects in this as given below.

Team-related Actions

The project manager needs to take actions that improve the effectiveness of the entire team as a single unit. Some of the actions undertaken are:

a) Setting team culture

b) Imparting training to team members

c) Organizing team building activities

d) Distributing rewards and recognition

Individual Actions

The project manager also needs to take actions in order to improve effectiveness of the individual team members. This includes conflict resolution, appraisals and motivation.

Conflicts are any kind of disagreement. They can be good if they bring out more creativity in the team, but if taken too far, can also become bad. A team without good conflicts is not very effective as all team members think in the same direction. The project manager should try to ask questions to the team in order to bring out different ideas, and, hence, conflict. If a conflict grows too much and starts affecting the project performance then it needs to be resolved. A project manager may take the following actions for resolving project conflicts:

a) Talk to individual team members in private. Analyze the situation and come to an acceptable resolution that is best for the project. Using such a technique does not make anybody feel bad as they know that the decision was taken in the best interest of the project. This is generally the best technique to use.

b) Try to arrive at a solution that would be a compromise. A compromise is an action taken where the solution may not be based on the merit of the situation, and, hence, may not be the best technique to use.

c) Use the project manager's position and arrive at a solution unilaterally and inform it to the parties in conflict without any further discussions. This kind of forced technique is not generally preferred unless the project is in a critical phase where time is precious.

d) The project manager may act as a catalyst in trying to resolve the conflict without actually taking part in its resolution. He would make the two parties aware of the points of agreement and coax them to get the same for points of disagreement. This kind of technique may not bring about a resolution.

The worst a project manager could do is to ignore the conflict altogether hoping that it would get resolved on its own. This rarely happens and then the project manager would have to resolve a heightened conflict sometime in future.

Appraisals are done in mainly three different ways in most companies. The first kind is where the boss appraises the sub-ordinate. It is a top-down approach as shown below:

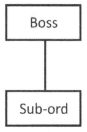

Several companies have realized that team members do not get much say in the appraisal process and feel they are at the receiving end. Hence, they have gone for an improved version where the sub-ordinates get a chance to appraise their bosses. This system is called reverse feedback. This is an inclusive way of doing appraisals that keeps a check on every individual from both, top and bottom. In most cases the sub-ordinate's feedback is actually sent to the boss's boss (higher management), who in turn uses it to do boss's appraisal as shown below:

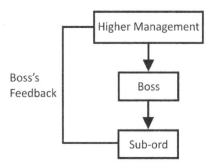

Yet other companies have implemented a 360 degrees feedback system where everybody appraises everybody who they work with, including customer and vendors. This ensures that everybody is appraised based on how they have performed from a 360 degrees view and not only in the view of their immediate boss or sub-ordinates. It is the most advanced form of appraisal that only some companies have been able to successfully implement. In order to implement this system, a change in company's culture is required wherein employees don't look at appraisals as an overhead but more as a means to enhance individual performance and get useful improvement feedback.

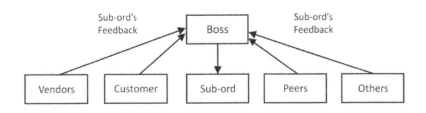

Motivation is an internal feeling within an individual that makes him like the work he does and increases his productivity. Project managers need to continually work on motivating their teams. One of the most accepted theories used to motivate knowledge workers (skilled workers) is the one given by Maslow. It is called Maslow's Hierarchy of Needs. This theory states that each individual has five levels of motivation as shown below:

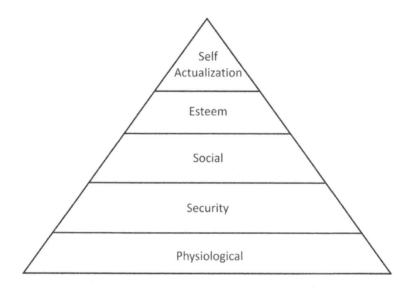

Each individual starts with the lowest level of motivation, Physiological level. This level is achieved when the person gets his basic needs satisfied – food, shelter, and clothing. Then he moves to the next level, Security, which is achieved with physical and job security. The next level, Social, is reached when the company makes the employee feel like an insider and there is a sense of belonging. When an individual reaches level 3 of motivation, in order to further motivate him his self esteem needs to be raised by giving more responsibility, recognition and the like. Finally, the last level is achieved by providing work that the person wants to do and by helping the person improve his knowledge through challenging assignments and trainings. Once at level 5, the person continues to be at that level as long as the project manager does enough to ensure that all levels under it exist. Otherwise the motivation comes down.

Project managers need to first determine the level at which each team member currently is. Then he needs to decide the course of action to take him to the next level above. For example, if a team member is at level 2 of motivation (security), the project manager might try to socialize more with this individual, involve him in decision making and make him feel a part of the team. This boosts him to level 3 of motivation (social). To further motivate him the project manager might decide to make him accountable for the work being carried out by a set of junior team members, effectively making this person the team leader. This promotes him to level 4 of motivation. Although the above steps sound easy, they have to be carefully thought of and executed and could take some time to show effect.

Quality Audits and Improvements

Projects make a quality plan that states the quality parameters that the project would achieve and the metrics (measurements) that would be collected in order to check the project's quality. Projects also undergo an audit at a set frequency to confirm that they are meeting the quality requirements in the plan and are also collecting the metrics to prove it.

Audits can be conducted either by internal experts or by external agencies. Almost every company has both. Internal audits are conducted at a set frequency of three to six months. External audits are conducted for certification/re-certification, like ISO 9001 certification audit.

An auditor is supposed to read the project's quality plan and ask for evidence proving that it is being followed. For example, if the plan says that a particular component would go through a round of testing once built, then the project should be able to provide documented evidence that the test was performed along with its results and corrective/preventive actions. An audit ends with the creation of an audit report that generally consists of three sections, non-conformances, observations, and suggestions/improvements. Given below is a sample audit report:

AUDIT REPORT

Project Name and Description

Project ABC. This project creates a website that provides access to company's existing and new customers.

Non-Conformances

a) The project does not have evidence showing a review that is mentioned in the quality plan under section 5. This review is to be performed when the login page is ready for testing. This is a **Minor** non-conformance.

b) Section 8 of the quality plan states that integration testing would be performed once all the pages have been tested individually before releasing the product. There is no evidence showing that this was done. This is a **Major** non-conformance.

Observations

a) Section 4 of the quality plan states that a test would be performed for the products page. The project has evidence showing that this test was performed but there is no evidence that the minor deviation in the test results was acted upon.

<u>**Suggestions/Improvements**</u>

a) The project can include in-process tests of individual web pages to reduce rework later on when the page is completed.

b) Peer review of development work can help in reducing the number of defects found in tests done later on.

A non-conformance is a major deviation from the quality plan and needs to be tracked to closure by taking appropriate action agreed upon between the auditor and the project manager. Observations are minor deviations that do not qualify for an outright non-conformance. These are not tracked to completion but if no action is taken, then the next time they may become a non-conformance. Suggestions are improvements suggested by the auditor to the project manager to do better in some areas that are already compliant.

Project Communications

Project Manager spends about 90% of his time communicating. Most of this is spent during project execution stage where he allocates work to team members, clarifies doubts, communicates with the customer to get details etc.

Lessons Learned should be created throughout the project and finalized and distributed to all stakeholders at a set frequency. Project generally share these either on a quarterly or half-yearly basis.

Stakeholder Management

While the project is being executed, stakeholders come up with issues related to the project. These are to be resolved by the project manager. It is best to log an issue as soon as it is known so that it can be tracked to completion. This also makes the stakeholder feel that the project manager cares for his issues and will try his best to get it to completion. All project issues are stored in an Issues Log that may look like the one given below:

Issue ID	Description	Raised By & When	Owner	Status	Expected Date of Completion	Resolution

Every issue is given a unique Issue ID and its details are put under the Description field. We also need to know the stakeholder who raised an issue so that clarifications, if any, can be sought. Hence, we store Stakeholder's name under Raised By along with the date when the issue was raised to know the age of the issue. Owner field stores the name of the person responsible to resolve the issue. Status specifies whether the issue is Open, Deferred, or Resolved. For all Open issues we also need to mention the Expected Date of Completion to track it to closure. If the issue has been resolved then the Resolution field stores the action taken to resolve it. This information helps resolving similar issues in future.

Below is a sample Issues Log with a few issues filled in:

Issue ID	Description	Raised By & When	Owner	Status	Expected Date of Completion	Resolution
1	Server keeps going down every hour	John 15th July 2012	Jack	Open	3rd Aug 2012	
2	Maria needs to work part-time in the month of Aug	Maria 20th July 2012	Mona	Resolved	25th July 2012	Mona has identified Joseph to take up Maria's work on the critical path
3	Customer wants to do early testing of login page	Customer 23rd July	Jack	Open	30th July 2012	

Procurement and Contracting

During the execution of the project contracts are signed with the vendors as and when required. The procurement documents are created for these during the project planning phase. During execution these documents are given to potential vendors. Sometimes the procurements are done in the public domain, wherein, any vendor may bid for the work. Vendors are generally informed through advertisements. Other times the company invites bids only from an approved list of vendors.

The procurement documents mention the details of the work to be performed in as much detail as possible. Even then the vendors may have queries before they submit their bids. Hence, a pre-bid meeting is organized where all the vendors are invited and there is a question and answer session driven by the project manager At the end of this meeting all the questions asked and answers given are documented and sent to all vendors so as to get a level playing field. Vendors then submit their bids and the bid evaluation process starts.

Procurement documents should carry the bid evaluation criteria so that vendors know on what basis their bids would be evaluated.

Bid Evaluation Criteria

These are the objective criteria that the project manager and his team would use to evaluate the various bids received in order to decide whom to award the contract. Commonly used criteria are as given below:

Screening System

Bids may be invited in two parts – technical bid and commercial bid. The technical bid is opened first and a decision is made based on how many bidders have the technical capability to perform the required job. Only the ones who qualify are moved to the next stage where commercial bids are opened. Commercial bids give the commercials quoted by the bidders and a ranking is established based on it, as L1, L2 etc. L1 is the lowest bid, L2 is the next in line and so on. The team may then decide to negotiate only with L1 and L2 and then award the contract on that basis.

Weighting System

In this system each bid is opened and rated on a scale (generally from 1-5) based on several parameters, like price, technical capability, financial stability, references of past work done etc. Each parameter is given a weight and the final figure arrives for each bidder. The bidder that gets the highest figure will be awarded the job. Alternatively, the company might decide to negotiate with the top two bidders before making a decision. Weighting system may look like the one shown below:

Parmeter	Weight	Bid-1		Bid-2		Bid-3	
		Rating	Weight × Rating	Rating	Weight × Rating	Rating	Weight × Rating
Price	30%	3	1	4	1.2	3	1
Technical strength	25%	5	1.25	4	1	3	0.75
Financial strength	20%	2	0.4	4	0.8	4	0.8
References	25%	3	0.75	4	1	5	1.25
Total			3.4		4		3.8

In the above example, the team might choose to award the contract to Bid-2 as they have the highest figure after applying the weighting system that was decided.

Independent Estimates

The project may also decide to take independent estimates either using the project's own capability or by employing outside consultants. This helps the project team to know what to expect in the bids. Consider an example where three bidders have submitted bids for the same work and they are $10 million, $50 million and $75 million. When the project team evaluates these bids they may not be able to say why the difference between the bids is so high unless they have some independent estimate to guide them. In this case, if the independent estimates state that the bids should be in the range of $40-$60 million then it is clear that the $10 million is too low and the bidder has probably not understood the requirement correctly. It also proves that the bidder who gave $75 million bid has over quoted. The only bidder in the expected range is the one who bid $50 million and, hence, might be the only one who has correctly understood the requirements.

Once the bids have been evaluated the project team chooses the vendor of their choice based on the evaluation criteria and negotiations. Then the contract is finalized and signed between the two parties. This completes the bidding process and the vendor starts working as per the conditions mentioned in the contract.

Solved Examples

4.1 As a project manager you need to decide the course of action to motivate a team member. You are sure that he has all the basic needs satisfied. He does not seem threatened about his job, and is able to work with other team members as a team. What can you do to motivate him?

Solution:

As per Maslow's Hierarchy of Needs, the first three levels are satisfied – physiological, security, and social. In order to bring greater motivation his self esteem needs to be raised. This can be done by giving more challenging responsibilities to the individual or by making him accountable for work being done by a set of juniors, effectively making him their manager. This will motivate the person to level 4.

4.2 The project team has received proposals for a piece of equipment to buy. They are unsure on how to make a selection between the proposals. Which of the following would help?

a) Price

b) Bid evaluation criteria

c) Contract

d) Expert opinion

Solution:

Bid evaluation criteria. These are the criteria that describe how bids would be evaluated.

4.3 What is the purpose of a quality audit?

Solution:

A quality audit helps the project manager understand the inefficient and ineffective practices being used on a project. The outcome of the audit is an audit report that provides inputs to the project manager on which processes are not being followed, and which processes can be improved further. A quality audit keeps a check on the overall project process adherence and gives a view on how compliant it is against the plan for the project.

Practice Exercise

4.1 Which of the following should appear in an Issues Log?

a) Name of Project Manager

b) Issue importance

c) Relation between issue and the project

d) Name of Issue Owner

4.2 Describe the importance of using Weighting System while evaluating bids.

4.3 A team member has been a consistent high performer and you would like to motivate him further to get the highest productivity. He has been assigned a lot of responsibilities that he is willingly performing. What can you do to motivate him further?

4.4 Describe the best way to resolve a conflict between two team members.

Solutions to the above questions can be downloaded from the **Online Resources** *section of this book on* **www.vibrantpublishers.com**

Chapter Summary

◆ Execution starts with resource mobilization, so that the project activities can be performed as planned.

◆ During execution, several team management actions need to be performed, like setting team culture, organizing trainings and organizing team building activities, and distributing rewards and recognitions.

◆ Conflict management is an important aspect of managing individual resources. Appraisals are also to be done in order to provide feedback to team members and also to provide data to the human resource department for pay hikes and promotions. Team member are motivated using different ways, most commonly by using the Maslow's Hierarchy of Needs theory.

◆ Quality Audits are performed at a set frequency on the project, to ensure that the project's processes are appropriate.

◆ Communications are done with all stakeholders in order to resolve their issues. Issue Log is maintained for this purpose. Lessons Learned is also collected throughout the project.

◆ If procurements are to be done, then vendors are invited to bid and contracts are signed with them. For evaluating the most appropriate vendor, screening system and weighting system are used. Independent Estimates may also be used to provide a reference for comparison of bids

Chapter **5**

Project Monitoring and Controlling

While the project is being executed, it also needs to be checked whether the execution is happening as per the plan. A project manager spends most of his time in execution, monitoring and controlling a project. Having a good, workable plan is one thing and being able to execute as per it is another. In several instances the execution does not happen as per the plan and this leads to issues later on. This is a monitoring and controlling failure on the project.

Monitoring

As the project is being executed, data is collected on the actual – actual scope delivered, actual start and end dates, actual costs incurred, actual quality measurements. All these are then compared with the ones mentioned in the plan. This difference is called Variance. If there is no variance then the project execution is happening as per the plan. If there is a variance then we need to do further analysis to see if the variance is a favourable one or an unfavourable one. For example, if an activity finished one day early then it is a favourable variance. On the other hand, if it finished one day late then it is an unfavourable variance that may warrant a response.

Control

When we determine that a particular variance is unfavourable then we may need to take an action to bring the project back on track. This action is called corrective action and is a part of the Control function. It may be possible that an unfavourable variance may not warrant a response at all. For example, if an activity is delayed for two days but it is not on the critical path and has ten days of float then a response may not be needed. There are also cases when the variance is within limits and, hence, does not warrant a response but we decide to take a preventive action to avoid issues in future. For example, one of the quality parameters in a construction activity is the strength of the concrete constructed. Let's say that the strength has a range from 1-10 and the acceptable range is 8-10. If the tests show that we are just at 8 then it may not warrant a response but we may still decide to take a preventive action so that future concretes fall closer to 9 or 10 and reduce the chance of having to take corrective action for them. The two types of actions – corrective and preventive actions, are often referred to as CAPA (corrective and preventive actions).

Schedule and Cost Tracking

The two most important areas to track on a project are schedule and cost. During planning the project schedule is base lined and so is the cost.

Variances

While executing, the actual values are collected and compared against the baseline and a variance is computed. The most important variances computed are as given below:

Schedule Variance (SV) – This is the difference between the baseline finish date and the actual finish date of an activity or the entire project.

Cost Variance (CV) – This is the difference between the baseline cost and the actual cost of an activity or the entire project.

Effort Variance (EV)/Work Variance – This is the difference between the baseline effort and actual effort spent on an activity or the entire project.

There are also some other variances that could be tracked at an activity level that give a greater degree of granularity as below:

Start Variance – This is the difference between the baseline start date and the actual start date of an activity.

Finish Variance – This is the difference between the baseline finish date and the actual finish date of an activity. It is similar to SV but only at an activity level.

Consider the example below that gives the baseline schedule and costs along with actuals. The variances are also calculated.

Parameter	Activity-1	Activity-2	Activity-3
Baseline			
Finish Date	1st August 2012	15th August 2012	5th Sept 2012
Cost	$20,500	$10,250	$60,025
Effort	10 Man Days	3 Man Days	25 Man Days
Actual			
Finish Date	1st August 2012	17th August 2012	4th Sept 2012
Cost	$20,500	$9,000	$62,025
Effort	10 Man Days	3.25 Man Days	23 Man Days
Variances			
SV	-	2 days	-1 day
CV	-	-$1,250	$2,000
EV	-	0.25 Man Days	-2 Man Days

In the above example Activity-1 has no variances as it completes as per schedule, with the same effort and spending as per baseline.

Activity-2 completes 2 days late, with 0.25 man days of extra effort and spending $1,250 less than baseline. It seems like this activity used a resource or materials of lower cost than planned.

Activity-3 completes 1 day early, with 2 man days of lower effort, and spending $2,000 more than baseline. It seems like this activity was completed faster by employing costlier resources.

Earned Value Technique

This is a technique used to track a project's progress based on cost parameters. It helps calculate both schedule and cost variances but gives all values in terms of costs.

Let's take an example of a project of painting four walls of equal size of a room. The project has been estimated to take 4 days and costs $40,000 (includes resource and material costs).Each wall takes $10,000 to complete and is planned to be done in 1 day. This project has been started and work has been done for 2 days. At the end of 2ⁿᵈ day we want to compute the variances to understand how the project is progressing. Below are some of the numbers we gather from our plan:

Parameter	Value	Description
Budget At Completion (BAC)	$40,000	Total budget of the project
Planned Value (PV)	$20,000	Budgeted value of the work planned in 2 days

We find out that only 1.5 walls have been painted so far and the actual cost incurred so far is $25,000 as shown below:

Parameter	Value	Description
Earned Value (EV)	$15,000	Budgeted value of work completed in 2 days
Actual cost (AC)	$25,000	Amount of money actually spent

We can now calculate SV and CV as below:

Parameter	Formula	Value
Schedule Variance (SV)	EV-PV	-$5,000
Cost Variance (CV)	EV-AC	-$10,000

It may be noted that any negative sign in this technique is construed as a bad sign. So the SV of -$5,000 actually means that we are behind schedule and the CV of -$10,000 means that we are over budget. We often compute the schedule and cost value in terms of ratios for better representation as below:

Parameter	Formula	Value
Schedule Performance of Index (SPI)	EV/PV	0.75
Cost Performance Index (CPI)	EV/AC	0.6

SPI says that we are going at 75% of originally planned rate and CPI states that for every $1 we invest we are only getting 60 cents back from the project.

From the above calculation it looks like we are going to be over budget but don't know by how much. So we calculate the revised budget a below:

Parameter	Formula	Value
Estimate At Completion (EAC)	BAC/CPI	$6,666.67

While computing the revised budget we have assumed that CPI will be constant throughout the project. This means that we would continue spending at the same rate. However, it may not always be the case. In this example if the materials (paint, brush etc.) were procured at the beginning of the project then the spending would be less towards the later part of the project as it would only be for the manpower. In such a case we use a modified formula for EAC as below:

Parameter	Formula	Value
Estimate At Completion (EAC)	AC + ETC	$45,000

ETC stands for Estimate To Complete. This is the estimated amount to be spent on the project from now until the end of the project. In our example it is the amount of manpower cost to paint the rest of the 2.5 walls as the materials have already been procured. It has been estimated above that the remaining manpower cost, ETC = $20,000.

Project Reporting

In the communications planning stage we have defined the type and frequency of reports to be sent to stakeholders. These reports are prepared after the project tracking information is available as part of project monitoring.

Project performance reports can have various forms of data. These are generally standardized for a particular company. Irrespective of what form they take the following sections would be present in some form:

Executive Summary

This section describes the brief summary of the report.

Project Activity

This section details out the activities along with their start, finish, and variance status, along with some comments to describe the variances.

Risk Update

This section describes any new risks or update on current risks that are currently impacting the project.

There are various kinds of reports sent on projects. These are described below:

Status Report

This is a cumulative report of all project activities from the beginning of the project until today. It is a long report and, hence, not sent very frequently. The preferred frequency is once a month or once a fortnight.

Progress Report

This is a report of the progress of activities from the last time the report was sent. For example, if this report is sent weekly then it would have the report of work done during the week. If it is sent daily then it will report only what happened during the day.

Trend Report

This is a summary report that shows a line graph of some project parameter. Just by looking at the trend one can infer whether the project is in good health or not. Below is one such trend about the SPI of the project:

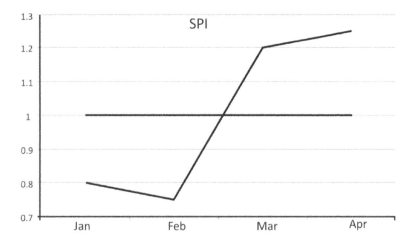

The trend above clearly shows that SPI of the project has been steadily increasing since Feb. This information is enough to infer that the project is going ahead of schedule. Similarly, if we include other trends, like CPI, Defects, etc. then we can say that the project is going smoothly on all fronts.

Variance Report

This is yet another summary report that gives the variances as below:

Schedule Variance (SV): 0.9

Cost Variance (CV): 1.1

The data above tells us that the project is behind schedule and under budget. With this information we may dig further into the progress and status reports to find the reason for delay.

Forecasting/Look-ahead Report

This report describes the activities that would be performed in future – 1 week look-ahead, 1 month look-ahead etc.

MIS (Management Information System) Report

This report is generally for internal consumption within the company and contains almost all the reports mentioned so far. It gives enough information to the company's senior management to take informed decisions.

Quality Control

While a deliverable is being prepared and once it is ready, it is generally subjected through a series of checks. These are in the form of reviews, inspections, and testing. These are called quality control checks. They are to verify that the deliverable meets the requirements mentioned in the plan.

It is best to perform quality control checks at stages within the process when the deliverable is not completely ready. These are called in-process quality control and help identifying quality issues earlier than later. This helps in reducing rework effort and cost. When a defect is found it is best to analyze the situation before resolving the bug in order to come up with a solution that will serve the project better in the long run. The tools mentioned in the sections below help in doing this analysis.

Ishikawa/Fishbone/Cause and Effect Diagram

This is tool used to get to the root cause of an issue. It is always best to get to the root cause and fix it, rather than fix the symptom. For example, when we visit a doctor with fever he does not directly treat the fever. He tries to diagnose the underlying root cause that is causing the fever – a symptom, and treats that. A fishbone diagram is drawn with the issue on the right and probable causes on the left usually using a brainstorming session. Below is an example of a fishbone diagram for an issue involving too many defects on the project.

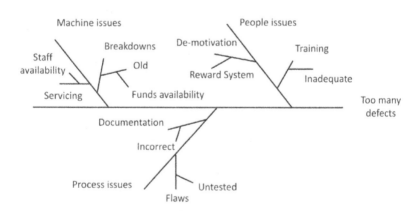

In the above fishbone diagram there are three major reasons for too many defects – People issues, Process issues, and Machine issues.

People issues can be due to Training or De-motivation. Training issue can be due to inadequate training provided and demotivation is due to non-existent or an unattractive rewards system.

Process issues can be caused due to issues with the process (flaws) or documentation of the process. Flaws could arise as the process might not be tested and documentation issues could be due to errors in the documentation.

Similarly, machine issues can be due to servicing or frequent breakdowns. Servicing issues can arise due to unavailability of servicing staff and breakdowns could be due to an old machine. The old machine is still in use due to lack of funds for buying a new one. The causes at the leaf (lowest) level are called root cause and the team determines the one that they think best fits the situation. Then efforts are directed towards fixing the root cause in order to reduce the issues.

Pareto Chart

It is always best to collect data related to the actual cause of issues and then prioritise them to know the top causes of issues. Pareto Chart helps in analyzing issues by plotting issues against their frequency of occurrence as below:

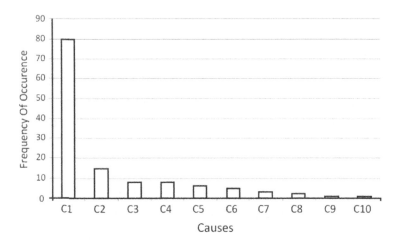

The causes are shown along the x-axis with the top causes on the left in descending order. Then the 80/20 rule is applied to the data so as to concentrate only on the top 20% causes. The 80/20 rule states that 80% of the problems are caused due to 20% of the underlying causes. So if we eliminate the top 20% of the causes we should expect 80% problems to go away. In the above Pareto chart we would concentrate our attention only on the top 2 causes – C1 and C2 and take action to fix them. This should help us getting rid of about 80% of the issues.

Risk Monitoring

Risks come from uncertainties that keep changing while the project is being executed. No matter how well risk planning has been done, one can always identify new risks during execution. Risk identification is a continuous process that happens throughout the project. Once a new risk has been identified, it also needs to be analyzed to understand its severity and respond to the risk.

The risks that were included in the risk register earlier can also be re-analyzed as some of them might not be there anymore, whereas, others might have become less or more severe than earlier. For example, if a risk identified on the project during planning was that there could be delays in getting approvals and the approvals have already come then this risk could be removed from the risk register now. Similarly, another risk identified was about labour unavailability and was earlier thought to be less severe but with time it appears to be more severe as it happens more often. This reanalysis of risks is called risk auditing.

There are some risks that are never identified but may still happen. They are then called issues and a workaround needs to be implemented at once. For example, if a critical resource falls sick and there is a delivery planned for today, the project manager needs to take immediate action by either identifying a replacement to do the work or informing the client that there would be delay in delivery.

Gaining Acceptance

As soon as a deliverable is ready it is shown to the customer and an acceptance is sought. The customer would either inspect the deliverable and/or run tests to ascertain whether it is as per the requirement. These tests would be mentioned in the acceptance criteria of the deliverable in the WBS dictionary. If the acceptance criteria are met the customer provides a written sign-off. Else he asks for rework.

It is important to take all sign-offs by the end of each phase of the project to avoid too much rework later on. There are times when a quality check as part of project's quality control effort fails. In such a case the project should not deliver the deliverable to the customer without rework. However, at other times the customer is in urgent need of the deliverable and is willing to give an exception and sign-off the deliverable as it satisfies his current need.

Managing Contracts

Once contracts have been signed during project execution the project manager ensures that all the contract terms and conditions are upheld by both parties to the contract. The project manager needs to ensure that his team does not violate any contract condition. If there is a breach of contract from the seller then a letter of default needs to be sent to them that mentions the breach along with corrective action to be taken.

During this time invoices are raised by the seller and paid by the buyer. Those invoices which the buyer does not agree with are called claims. Payments are processed as per the contract terms. The buyer also conducts audit of the seller's process at a set frequency to ensure that they are following the agreed upon process. The seller sends performance reports to the buyer at the decided frequency. Deliverables are given by the seller and accepted by the buyer – sign-off of deliverables is given by the buyer.

Handling Changes

Changes are a reality in projects. These are asked by the stakeholders as they add more value to them. However, too many changes are not good as they lead to rework, frustration, and increased cost. Changes are also difficult to implement towards the later stage of the project. For example, if the change requires the project's design to be modified then it would be too costly and difficult to implement such a change once the development is almost complete.

If the project manager fails to identify all stakeholders in the project's initial phase then changes could be detected later on when these stakeholders become aware of the project and give their requirements. Changes may also come from stakeholders due to their business needs, market changes, regulatory changes, or any other factor that was not known when the initial requirements were frozen.

It is best to anticipate changes and keep a change control process ready to handle changes as and when they come. A good change control process should have the following elements:

a) **Change Request Template** – this is a standard form that needs to be filled in by the requester of the change. It contains those items that are needed by the team to analyze and include the change in the project's scope.

b) **Change Request SPOC** – this is a representative of the team who acts as a single point of contact (SPOC) for changes requested to the project. The outside stakeholders should not be allowed to give changes to all team members as it could lead to chaos. It is always good to allocate a single person who should be taking change requests.

c) **Impact Analysis Team** – this is a list of people who would be responsible to analyze all change requests and forward their analysis to the approving authority.

d) **Approving Authority** – this is the name(s) of one or more stakeholders who would take a decision on whether the requested change should be included or not.

Following is the process to be followed for all requested changes:

a) **Feasibility Study** – is it technically possible to implement the requested change?

b) **Impact Analysis** – how does the change impact the project's schedule, cost, risk, resources and quality?

c) **Determining Options** – what are various ways this change can be implemented?

d) **Getting Approval** – presenting the analysis and recommendations to the approving authority of the project.

Solved Examples

5.1 A project has been estimated to cost $150,000. It was planned to complete work worth $50,000 until today but work actually completed is worth $45,000. We have already spent $48,000 so far on the project. What is the project's SPI and CPI? What is the meaning of these values?

Solution:

BAC = $150,000

PV = $50,000

EV = $45,000

AC = $48,000

SPI = EV/PV = $45,000/$50,000 = 0.9

CPI = EV/AC = $45,000/$48,000 = 0.94

SPI of 0.9 means that we are progressing at 90% of the originally planned rate

CPI of 0.94 means that for every $1 of investment on the project we are only getting work worth 94 cents

5.2 Defect data has been collected on a project. The project team is trying to determine how they can improve quality. The data is as shown below:

Defect Cause	Number of Defects
Incorrect process documentation	5
Human error	1
Machine error	45
Inadequate testing	2
Process adherence	10

Solution:

Since data of causes is available we should use it to create a Pareto Chart and determine the top causes. Then we should resolve top 20% of the causes.

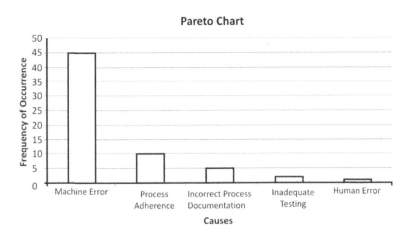

Applying 80/20 rule we should only concentrate on the top cause – Machine error.

5.3 The customer has asked for a change in the scope of the project. The project manager has analyzed the change to check feasibility. What is the NEXT thing to do?

    a)   Ask the customer if there are more changes

    b)   Implement the change immediately

    c)   Present the analysis to the customer

    d)   Analyze the impact of the change on project schedule and cost

Solution:

Analyze the impact of the change on project schedule and cost

Practice Exercise

5.1 Which of the following reports provides a bird's eye view to the project stakeholders?

   a) Status report

   b) Progress report

   c) Variance report

   d) Forecasting report

5.2 The following values have been collected on a project:

BAC = $1 million

PV = $300,000

EV = $400,000

AC = $390,000

Calculate CPI and EAC if the performance is expected to be the same throughout the project

5.3 What are the various variances that are tracked on the project?

5.4 What is the difference between preventive and corrective actions?

Solutions to the above questions can be downloaded from the **Online Resources** *section of this book on*
www.vibrantpublishers.com

Chapter Summary

- Monitoring of a project is done in order to check if it is going as per plan. This is effectively done by computing variances – schedule and cost variances are most common.

- Controlling of a project is done by taking appropriate corrective and preventive actions.

- Earned Value (EV) Technique can be used to track project variances. The important parameters computed in this technique are SV, CV, SPI, and CPI.

- Project performance reports, like status report and progress report, are shared with the stakeholders to inform them of the project's health.

- Ishikawa diagram and Pareto chart are used when issues arise on a project. The prior is used for root cause analysis, and the latter for prioritization of causes.

- Risk monitoring is a continuous effort. It involves identification of new risks, closure of existing risks, and changing, re-analyzing, or re-prioritizing of existing risks.

- Deliverables are also validated by the customer and acceptances received throughout the project.

- Project has to be monitored against all its contracts, to ensure that there is no breach and all the terms and conditions of the contracts are adhered to. Changes have to be handled as they are identified. Every project should have a change request template, changes, impact evaluation team, and analysis, before the options are presented to the approval authority.

This page is intentionally left blank

Chapter **6**

Project Closure

Once all the work on the project has been completed it must be closed. Project closure is often skipped by the project team as they are busy celebrating the end of the project or get busy executing other projects. However, this stage has great importance. The importance lies in three ways – getting formal acceptance on the project, computing project profitability, and utilizing the learning in future projects.

If a project misses to take formal acceptance then there could be problems later on, wherein, the stakeholders may say that the project work was not completed as per their expectations. It is always best to take such an acceptance in writing. When a project is selected, the company computes the expected cash flows that the project would generate and selects the project only if it seems profitable. However, it is necessary to check the project profitability at closure to see if it matches with what was anticipated. This helps the company take better project selection decisions in future. Every project has learning that can be applied to other projects in future. Unless these are documented they would be lost over time. During project closure there are two main stages – closure of the project's contracts and closure of the project itself.

Closing Contracts

Every project has a contract with the customer. It may also have additional contracts with vendors, suppliers, and sub-contractors. The first stage in closure is to ensure that all the terms and conditions of all these contracts have been met as these have legal significance. The project manager is expected to go through all the items in all the project's contracts and confirm that they have been met. For vendor, supplier, sub-contractor contracts the project manager should send a work completion certificate to inform the sellers that their job has been done as per the contract's terms and conditions.

Once all of the project's contracts with sellers have been closed the contract with the customer needs to be closed. For this, the project manager needs to approach the customer and ask for a work completion certificate. He may be asked to make a project closure report and present it to the stakeholders to convince them that all work has been completed. All the project's payments have to be processed. If there is a warranty period then all the project documents are handed over to the operations team that would look after the product during its warranty period.

Closing Project

Once the project's contracts have been closed it becomes a stand-alone entity that can be closed. The most important thing that needs to be done during this time is creation of Lessons Learned. This is a document that specifies what went well and what went wrong on the project. The things that went well can be repeated on future projects, whereas, the things that went wrong are to be avoided on future projects. All project's documents are archived for future reference and form part of the company's repository of historical data. This data can be used by project managers on future projects to plan their project. For example, similar projects in future may use the risk register from the project to identify risks on their project.

Solved Examples

6.1 What are the benefits of making Lessons Learned?

Solution:

Lessons Learned have the following benefits:

a) They tell us what are the things that went well so we should continue doing those on future projects

b) They tell us what are the things that did not go well so we should avoid them on future projects

c) They provide historical information that can be used for planning future projects

6.2 What should be done while closing contracts on a project?

Solution:

The project manager should go through all the terms and conditions of the contract to ensure that they have been completed. Work completion certificate should be given to sellers and taken from the customer of the project.

Practice Exercise

6.1 Which of the following is NOT done during project closure?

    a)   Creating Lessons Learned

    b)   Getting project sign-off

    c)   Releasing team members

    d)   Getting sign-off of deliverables

6.2 Why should contracts on a project be closed before creating Lessons Learned?

Solutions to the above questions can be downloaded from the **Online Resources** *section of this book on*
www.vibrantpublishers.com

Chapter Summary

◆ When a project has completed all the work, it needs to be formally closed. This starts with the closure of all its contracts – with the customer as well as with the suppliers.

◆ While closing supplier contracts, we need to ensure that all the work expected from them has been delivered, and then a work completion certificate needs to be issued to them. Similarly, when closing contract with the customer, we need to get a work completion certificate from the customer.

◆ Lesson Learned are collated and shared with the relevant parties. A Project Closure Report may also be prepared to present the project's success/failure to the stakeholders.

This page is intentionally left blank

Glossary

Activity Attributes – provides details of the activities on a project. Generally stored in the form of a one-page document for each activity.

Actual Cost (AC) – amount of money actually spent in performing the work so far

Bar Chart – a diagram that shows the project activities along with their dependencies in a diagrammatic form, generally against a timeline/calendar. It can also show progress for each activity.

Baseline – an approved plan against which the project actual results are compared

Brainstorming – a group technique where diverse ideas are encouraged in order to come up with the best solution or to make a list of possible causes or risks

Budget At Completion (BAC) – the total estimated budget of the project at the beginning

Checklist – a list of company and/or industry specific items that are used to remind the project to perform a set of activities

Conflict – a kind of disagreement that may lead to a better solution and creativity if managed well

Constraint – hindrances, roadblocks or limits given to the project manager within which the project needs to be managed

Contingency Reserve – a reserve kept in the project's budget to take care of known risks

Contract – a legal agreement between the customer and the project or between the project and its vendors/suppliers/sub-contractors

Corrective Action – the action taken when the project's performance does not match with the plan

Cost of Quality – the total amount of money spent on quality on a project

Cost Performance Index (CPI) – EV/AC. This parameter shows whether the project is within budget, on budget, or over budget. CPI < 1 means over budget, CPI = 1 means on budget, and CPI > 1 means under budget.

Cost Plus/Cost Reimbursable (CR) – ya type of contract where the seller is reimbursed for the actual costs incurred by him plus an additional amount is paid as profit

Cost Variance (CV) – EV – AC. This parameter shows whether the project is within budget, on budget, or over budget. CV < 0 means over budget, CV = 0 means on budget, and CV > 0 means under budget.

Crashing – a schedule compression technique where resources are added to complete the project faster

Critical Path – the longest path in the network diagram that determines the end date of the project

Critical Path Method (CPM) – a method used to identify the critical path of the project using the project's network diagram, to calculate float, and early and late start and finish dates of all project activities

Decomposition – the action of breaking down project work into smaller pieces in the WBS

Deliverable – a part of the project's product that can be independently given to the customer to get a sign-off

Direct Cost – those costs which are directly incurred on the project and, hence, can be easily traced to the particular project

Duration – the total number of days (or elapsed days or calendar days) that will be taken by an activity or the project

Early Finish (EF) – the earliest date by when an activity on a project can be finished

Early Start (ES) – the earliest date by when an activity on a project can be started

Earned Value (EV) – the planned value of the work actually accomplished on a project

Effort – the man hours/days required to complete an activity or the project

Estimate At Completion (EAC) – the revised budget (BAC) while the project is being executed. Give by either BAC/CPI or AC + ETC.

Estimate To Complete (ETC) – the value of the remaining work on the project

Fast Tracking – a schedule compression technique where more project activities are done in parallel

Finish-to-Finish – a type of dependency between project activities where the finish of an activity depends on the finish of another activity

Fixed Price (FP)/Lumpsum – a type of contract where the seller quotes a lumpsum price for performing the work defined by the buyer

Finish-to-Start – a type of dependency between project activities where the start of an activity depends on the finish of another activity

Float – the amount of time an activity can be delayed without delaying the project

Gantt Chart – a diagram that shows the project activities along with their dependencies in a diagrammatic form, generally against a timeline/calendar. It can also show progress for each activity.

Indirect Cost – the overhead costs that the project incurs which cannot be directly traced to the project. These costs are generally apportioned to the project.

Lag – the waiting time between activities

Late Finish (LF) – the latest date by when an activity on a project should be finished

Late Start (LS) – the latest date by when an activity on a project should be started

Lead – the amount of time an activity is started earlier than its start date to expedite the project. It is exactly opposite of lag. When taking a lead, there would be an overlap between two activities that have a dependency.

Lessons Learned – a document that describes the learning from the project (both good and bad) that can be applied to similar projects in future

Management Reserve – a reserve kept in the project's budget to take care of unknown risks

Management By Objectives (MBO) – a way of managing a company, wherein, objectives are set for all personnel and their actual performance is evaluated against these objectives

Milestone – a significant achievement. It is denoted in the form of a date and it does not have any effort/duration of its own.

Operations – repetitive work done that is not categorized as a project

Parametric Estimate – an estimate that is based on some parameter/unit and which is calculated using a thumb-rule from historical data

Pareto Chart – a chart that is used to show a prioritized list of causes of an issue. Only the top 20% of the causes are acted upon as per the 80/20 rule.

Program Evaluation And Review Technique (PERT) – an estimation technique that uses three estimates – Optimistic, Most Likely, and Pessimistic, in order to arrive at a final estimate. This is used when there is uncertainty in the work due to which it is difficult to arrive at a single estimate.

Planned Value (PV) – the value of the work planned to be done on the project

Portfolio – a collection of projects, programs, and operations that share the same strategic objectives

Preventive Action – the action taken when the project's performance matches with the plan but is very close to being beyond the acceptable range. If no action is taken, the performance would soon be out of the acceptable range.

Program – a collection of related projects being managed in a co-ordinated way

Project – any work being done that has a start and end date and that gives a unique outcome

Project Charter – a document that authorizes a project

Project Management Office (PMO) – a centralized department that builds the company's capabilities in project management

Project Plan – a document that states how the project would be executed. It includes all parts of a project – scope, time, cost, quality, human resource, communications, risk, procurement.

Q

uality – conformance to requirements

R

ate Contract – a type of contract where the buyer and seller agree on a rate card for a particular type of resource on a per hour/per day basis. The invoicing is done based on the actual resource usage.

Resource Histogram – a bar chart showing the resource usage on a project over time

Rework – work done to fix a defect found on a project

Risk – an event that has an uncertainty in its occurrence and has an impact on the project

Risk Acceptance – a type of risk response where the consequences of the risk are knowingly accepted

Risk Avoidance – a type of risk response where action is taken such that the risk no longer exists on the project

Risk Mitigation – a type of risk response where action is taken such that the severity of the risk on the project is reduced

Risk Register – a document that stores the project's risks, their analysis, and responses taken

Risk Transfer – a type of risk response where action is taken such that the risk is transferred to a third party – a vendor, an insurance company etc.

Root Cause – the underlying cause of an issue, which when fixed will fix the issue

Start-to-Finish – a type of dependency between project activities where the finish of an activity depends on the start of another activity

Start-to-Start – a type of dependency between project activities where the start of an activity depends on the start of another activity

Time and Material Contract – a type of contract where the buyer and seller agree on a rate card for a particular type of resource on a per hour/per day basis. The invoicing is done based on the actual resource usage.

Variance – the difference between the actual results and the baseline (plan)

Variance At Completion (VAC) – BAC – EAC. This parameter shows the total variance of the project budget. VAC < 0 means over budget, VAC = 0 means on budget, and VAC > 0 means under budget.

Work Breakdown Structure (WBS) – a hierarchical structure where the project is broken down (decomposed) into smaller pieces as we go down the hierarchy

WBS Dictionary – a one-page document that describes a work package

Work Package – the smallest piece of work that lies at the bottom-most level of the WBS

Workaround – action taken during project execution when an issue occurs that was not identified earlier as a risk

NOTES

NOTES

Made in the USA
Coppell, TX
07 February 2021